Date Due

STRATEGIES FOR
THE OPTIONS TRADER

STRATEGIES FOR
THE OPTIONS TRADER

CLAUD E. CLEETON

A WILEY-INTERSCIENCE
PUBLICATION

JOHN WILEY & SONS

New York • Chichester
Brisbane • Toronto

Library of Congress Cataloging in Publication Data

Cleeton, Claud Edwin, 1907–
   Strategies for the options trader.

   "A Wiley-Interscience publication."
   Bibliography: p.
   Includes index.
   1. Put and call transactions. I. Title.

HG6041.C53   332.6′45   78-11230
ISBN 0-471-04973-5

Printed in the United States of America

10 9 8 7 6 5 4 3 2 1

Preface

This book is a complete options manual for the options trader. It describes stock options and discusses their various uses. Techniques, charts, and tables provide the tools for evaluating options, selecting strategies, and the timing of transactions. Examples and charts provide practical illustrations, not idealized situations.

Formulas for normal values of puts and calls cover all market conditions. The concept of option volatility is developed, which permits price evaluation of individual options as to being over- or under-priced and allows comparisons to be made indicating the pricing level of options as a whole.

The various option strategies are analyzed, and charts show you where in price and when in time to take action for maximum profit potential. Option prices vary mainly because the underlying stock price changes. Short-term timing and prediction methods are described for picking the stocks offering the best option trading situations, and you are shown how to find the buy and sell signals for the individual stocks and the stock market as a whole.

Normal values for option price and volatility may be computed using the formulas, and programs are given for making the computations on the small hand-held calculators. As an alternative, unique universal option tables are provided that may be used to "look up" these values with an accuracy that may be selected to meet any practical need.

My thanks go to my wife, Mary Ellen, for editing and proofreading assistance.

CLAUD E. CLEETON

Washington, D.C.
November 1978

Contents

nations • Combining stock with options • A final word

STRATEGIES FOR
THE OPTIONS TRADER

1 The Options Market

—Before you start
To play the game, you need a guide

If someone owns something you think you might want to buy, you may be able to reach an agreement with this person (or owner) to sell it to you at some later time at an agreed price, if you decide you want it. It is said that you have purchased an *option* on this asset, which might be a piece of property, a stock, or any other type of asset. For the privilege of taking time to make up your mind, or for some other reason, such as having to wait until funds are available, you pay the owner some money that is his to keep even though you may later decide not to make the purchase. The seller of the option considers this payment a reimbursement for keeping the asset available to deliver to you as long as the option was agreed to exist. This is an option to purchase.

Conversely, if you own an asset, you may pay another a sum of money for which he agrees to purchase your asset at an agreed price within a specified length of time, if you decide to sell. The payment reimburses him for holding funds available to make the purchase, if you so decide. This is an option to sell. Options can apply to almost anything, but we will limit further considerations to common stocks and related securities.

If you are to understand the options market and be able to communicate in it, you need to become familiar with some specialized terms not normally used in the ordinary stock market vocabulary. This chapter serves to orient you in the options game.

WHAT IS A STOCK OPTION?

A *stock option* is a contract to purchase or to sell a stock at a stated price within a specified time. There are two types of stock options, *puts* and *calls*. A call is a stock option to buy, typically 100 shares, of the underlying stock at a stated price, called the *striking price* or *exercise price*, within a specified time period; that is, ownership of a call gives you the privilege of calling (buying) 100 shares of the stock from the seller of the call at the striking price, within the specified time period. A put is the reverse of a call; that is, if you own a put, you have the privilege of putting to the seller of the put 100 shares of your stock for his purchase at the striking price, within the specified time period. The option on 100 shares of stock is referred to as one *option contract*.

Options are considered a capital asset, but they exist for limited times only. They have a specific expiration date and after this date are worthless. Because of this feature, options are a *wasting asset*. The option must be *exercised* prior to the expiration date, if there is to be a transfer of stock.

EXCHANGE-TRADED OPTIONS

Options on stocks have been available on the over-the-counter market for many years, but they did not incite wide interest until the Chicago Board Options Exchange (CBOE) was established and began trading in call options in April 1973. Their success encouraged other exchanges to add option trading to their services. In June 1977 trading started in put options. The number of stocks covered has built up on the various exchanges to give a wide variety and sufficient coverage to meet your desires.

Before the advent of the CBOE, options were bought or sold by bringing the two parties together to establish a mutually agreed contract. There was no secondary market in which one could dispose of an option at will. Options would usually be exercised at the desire of the holder or allowed to expire. The CBOE changed all this in April 1973 by establishing a secondary market in which you can buy and sell call options as you do a stock. The addition of put options in June 1977 completed the package. Prices are quoted, and you pay a commission in accordance with a schedule of fees. In addition to making available a secondary market in options, the options are standardized to have specified striking prices and expiration dates.

Since options are merely limited time contracts between a buyer and a seller of the contract, they are no part of the corporation whose stock is designated in the options contract. There are no certificates representing ownership, but simply a bookkeeping operation. The broker's confirmation is your record of the transaction. The Options Clearing Corporation issues options, clears closing transactions, and initiates action when exercise notices are received. When the same option is listed on more than one exchange, it may be bought on one and sold on another.

A *class* of options are those of the same type, put or call, covering the same underlying security. There is normally a minimum of two striking prices for each expiration date, and as the stock prices move up or down, other striking prices are added so that in some classes there may be several available striking prices. Three expiration times are established, separated by 3 months, and as one expiration date passes, new options are established with 9 months to expiration.

The *open interest* is the number of contracts in existence at a particular time. *Barron's* reports the open interest for each option weekly. The number is useful in judging the activity in a specific option. When trading, you want to have good liquidity.

PREMIUMS

The price of an option is called the *premium*. When the striking price of a call option is less than the price of the underlying stock, the premium is said to be *in the money*. It consists of two parts. One, the *intrinsic value*, is equal to the difference between the stock price and the striking price and is the part of the option value that makes up this difference if the call is exercised. The other part is called the *time value* and represents the value of the privilege to obtain the stock through exercise. The time value is larger for the longer times to expiration and vanishes at the expiration date. The time value accounts for the difference in option premiums of the same striking price but different times to expiration.

When the stock price is below the striking price, the call option is said to be *out of the money*. Such options have no intrinsic value but may trade at some value up to expiration. The smallest price unit is one-sixteenth of a point. When the stock price equals the striking price, the option is said to be *at the money*.

Similar terms are applied to put options, the price relations being the reverse. A put is in the money when the stock price is below the striking price; that is, a put has an intrinsic value equal to the extra amount you would get by putting your stock to the put seller over what you would get by selling at the market. When the stock price is above the striking price, a put sells out of the money.

OPENING AND CLOSING TRANSACTIONS

One may open an options position by either a purchase or a sale. This position may be liquidated in a closing transaction. The purchase of an option creates a long position. You pay the option price plus commissions in cash. You are in control of the situation. You may sell the option in the secondary market and liquidate your position when advantageous to do so. You may exercise your option at the striking price any time before it expires, purchasing stock if a call or selling stock if a put.

You may open a position by selling an option. This is similar to selling a stock short. In the options market it is frequently called *writing options*. If you own 100 shares of a stock for which there are exchange-traded calls, you can write (sell) a call against this stock. This is called *covered writing*. There is no margin required as long as you continue to hold the underlying stock. Securities that are convertible into shares of the underlying stock also serve to provide cover for covered writing. You need to know the conversion ratio and own enough of the convertible to cover 100 shares of the common for each option contract. The premium received for writing the call, after commissions, is immediately available to you. You can also write a call without owning the underlying stock. This is known as *uncovered writing* or *naked writing*. Unlike the short sale of stock, you do not have to borrow stock, since the option is merely a contract that can be created by the Options Clearing Corporation to satisfy the public demand. You do, however, have to meet existing margin requirements, which are established by federal regulations, plus anything additional that may be required by the exchange or your broker. Margin requirements are discussed further later.

When you write (sell) a put, you are obligated to purchase stock if the put is exercised. This transaction always involves margin. When you buy a put you may or may not own the stock. If you do own the stock, you will want to check the current tax laws because the purchase of a put may change your holding period. You may also be short in the stock, in which case you could exercise your put to cover your short stock at the striking price.

BROKERAGE ACCOUNTING

You need to be familiar with accounting terms used by the brokerage house, when trading options, if you are to keep track of your position. A *cash account* is the ordinary account with your broker, in which you can buy and sell stocks and bonds, paying for any you buy within the specified settlement period. You may withdraw any proceeds from sale of securities or from dividends and interest collected.

A *margin account* is one in which you are permitted to borrow, within specified percentage amounts, money from your broker, pledging your securities as *collateral*, on which borrowed funds you pay interest at a rate that varies from time to time; you have to get the exact rate from your particular broker. You need to establish a margin account for certain types of option transactions, even though you intend always to put up cash as required, and you have margin statements as well as regular account statements.

Whenever you purchase a security, including options, your account is *debited* for the cost. You have a *debit* entry on the account records, which is placed on the left-hand side, following bookkeeping practice. When you make payment for the purchase, a *credit* entry is entered on the right-hand side. If you sell a security, you receive a credit. If you withdraw money from your account, it is entered as a debit on your brokerage account.

In some kinds of option transactions, in which you simultaneously take a position in different options on the same underlying stock, you may want to give your order in terms of a debit or credit difference. In this way you specify your cost or credit without being concerned about the prices of the individual options, but rather their difference in price.

WHO NEEDS OPTIONS?

Options can be used in many ways. They can be used in a wide range of investment programs. Though they are basically speculative, they can be used in a very conservative program.

Perhaps the most common use, and the one most like the purchase of common stock, is the buying of calls rather than the purchase of the underlying stock with the view of achieving capital gains. Timewise you must be a trader, for the option has limited life. In general, if the stock is a good buy on a trading basis, there is a call that is a good buy, and when the stock is a sell, the call is a sell. The price of the option is directly related to the price of the underlying stock. It moves because the stock price moves. You must first analyze the stock movement and then select the best option for this stock. Why buy a call instead of the stock? Primarily for leverage and next for reduced risk. For an average-priced stock, the percentage gain in call value is several times the percentage gain in the stock price. The intrinsic value increases point for point, but the time value of the call decreases as time is consumed by the price advance. What do you pay for this leverage? A risk of losing your entire investment because the call may be worthless at a time in the future. It is not all this bad; when you buy the call, you know exactly how much you could lose if the worst comes to pass. You would never buy a stock thinking that one day it would be worthless, but the stock price could easily fall more than the total price of the call, and your inclination is to hold on, hoping for a comeback, only to lose even more. Good advice is to restrict your option funds to a small percentage of your investment funds and put the rest in safe cash equivalent, earning consistent interest, but always there if you need them. This program can be more conservative overall than putting all your money in common stocks.

If you like to play the short side in bear markets, options are a good substitute for selling stock short. You can buy puts instead, and you have some major advantages. You limit your risk, you have leverage, you do not have to borrow stock, and you do not have to pay dividends on borrowed stock. You can also short options by selling calls in a bear market and selling puts in a bull market, but you introduce unlimited risk. One compensating factor is that the time value of these options decreases and thus works with you.

There are some special situations not found in the market of common stocks. One of interest is the sale of out-of-the-money options when they have only a short time to expiration. The intent is to pick options almost certain to expire worthless; so you merely pocket the sale proceeds and let the position close itself out by expiration in a short span of time. These sales can be productive, even though the stock price does not change or even goes up somewhat, in the case of a call, as long as it does not exceed the striking price by expiration time or goes down, in case of a put, as long as it does not fall below the striking price.

Covered call writing may be used to increase the income from holdings of stocks. If you own stock and want to retain your position in it, you can sell calls against this stock. If the stock is expected to do nothing or decrease in price, you may be able to pick up a few hundred dollars several times a year by writing calls. If you purchase stock and sell a call that is somewhat out of the money and the stock should later be called, your profit is the sum of the premium received on the call and the difference between what you paid for the stock and its striking price, less all commissions. If the call is not exercised, you pocket the premium and write another call, etc., which can be several times a year. On average you may expect to gain perhaps 20% a year if followed consistently. You can write puts, if this seems more appropriate to the situation. Option selection is dealt with in more detail in later chapters.

Another reason to purchase an option is to establish the price of a stock transaction that you do not want to enter into at the moment. Suppose you wanted to buy 100 shares of a certain stock and did not have the cash now but knew you would be receiving funds in a few months, and you expected the stock to rise substantially by that time. You could buy a call having an expiration time at least as far in the future as the time you expected to have the funds to purchase the stock. This would establish the price you are going to pay for the stock (the striking price) and could well save you money if the stock does move upward as you expect.

On the other hand, you may own stock that you do not want to sell at this time, and you are uncertain about the market for the near term and want to protect yourself against a decrease in the stock price. You can purchase a put that gives you the privilege of selling your stock during the life of the put at the striking price and thus protect your stock price and profits against a loss due to a downward turn in the market. Also, you can write (sell) a call as protection against a decrease in stock price. The premium received serves to give you protection against an equal decrease in stock price.

Another use of options is to hedge a short sale of the underlying security. The purchase of a call gives you protection against an increase in the price of the stock; that is, it establishes the maximum price you would have to pay should you have to cover a short sale that went against you.

A put can be purchased to give your long position protection against a price decline. It establishes the minimum price you would receive if you desire to close out your position.

You may use options to protect your economic position and at the same time participate in future gains. If you own a stock having a long-term gain, you can sell the stock short against the box and buy a call. Your long-term gain on the stock is ensured, and the call allows you to participate in any futher increase in stock price, though such further gains would be short-term.

If you own a stock having a short-term gain, a call can be sold that will give some protection on the downside, and if its expiration date is far enough into the future for the stock gains to mature into long-term, you may wait for its exercise and realize long-term gains on both the stock and the proceeds of the call. If the stock price increases substantially, the call may be purchased to take a short-term loss while realizing long-term gains on the entire appreciation of the stock.

SOME WARNINGS

There are specific risks in trading in options. In purchasing an option for capital appreciation, you stand a chance of the price movement's going against you, as in any market transaction, but further you can quickly lose your entire investment because of the limited life of the option. You may not have the time to wait for a price reversal. Your timing must be reasonably accurate if you are to make profits consistently. If dealing in the near to expire options, the timing must be the most accurate.

When writing options, you are not in control, other than being able to liquidate your position by a closing transaction. As long as you hold this short position, you are subject to early exercise, which can cost you added commissions through having to buy and sell the underlying stock. Your broker may give you a break on the fast turnaround, thus reducing the cost somewhat. Although most options are not exercised early, but at or near the end of their life, it can happen, and you must be prepared in case it does. One reason, when procuring a large quantity of stock, calls may be purchased to establish the purchase price without significantly affecting the price of the stock or to establish the stock price while awaiting funds to purchase the stock. When these call holders are ready to purchase, they may do so rather than wait.

If writing options and you do not own the stock when selling the call or you are not short the stock when selling the put, the price of the stock may go against you, running up the price of the option you would have to purchase to close the position to stop the increasing losses.

When writing covered calls, you give up the opportunity for gain in the underlying stock as long as the call position is open. And if writing puts while holding a short position in the stock, you give up the opportunity to profit from a fall in price of the stock.

2 Normal Values

—What's an option worth?

The *normal value* of an option is the price one expects it to trade at under specified conditions if it is not overpriced or underpriced. It may be considered the average price for these specified conditions. A given set of conditions exists only for a brief time; so the normal value changes continuously. It changes with time so that the normal value on one day may be slightly different the next day, even though all other factors remain the same. During the day, if the underlying stock price changes, the normal option value changes. Thus, the normal value of an option is not a fixed price or even a simple thing to determine.

NORMAL VALUES ARE REFERENCE VALUES

At any given time, the quoted price of an option may agree well with a calculated normal value, or it may be less, said to be *undervalued*, or it may be priced higher than the calculated normal value, said to be *overvalued*. Remember the normal value is only an average. It does not necessarily provide a price at which an option can be bought or sold but rather provides a reference against which actual prices can be compared.

In some discussions on option pricing you may encounter the term *inefficient market*. If the option prices were always in the proper price relation to each other and priced correctly, it is said the option market is efficient. In an inefficient market, undervalued and overvalued situations arise.

Many advisory services and brokerage houses publish normal values in one form or another, and there is often considerable disagreement among them, depending to some extent on their computer programs and the individual data inputs. The formulas used in this book are derived by fitting equations to the average of actual quoted prices over a long period of time. Somewhat different results may be obtained if different data spans are used. Conditions do change, but these are largely taken care of by determining the option volatility value for the range of time of interest. In this manner, the normal values are adjusted to the period of time of interest, which can be very short, even comparing the various options of a single class for the day. Or an average value can be determined for periods of a few weeks, a year, etc. Moving averages may be used if desired.

DETERMINING NORMAL VALUES

There have been numerous studies on the pricing of options and warrants. A *warrant* is an option to purchase the stock of a corporation for a specified price. Warrants differ from exchange-traded call options in that the warrant is a liability of a corporation whose life is typically measured in years, rather than months, though some are perpetual. Otherwise they are quite similar. Various computer programs have been developed for computing the normal value of exchange-traded options in terms of the underlying stock price and time to expiration. Most of these involve such factors as the stock volatility, interest rates, dividends paid on the stock, and other elements that influence option prices. Some of these factors can only be estimated. Many such programs are based on the studies of Black and Scholes.*†

A somewhat different approach has been taken, and formulas for computing normal values have been derived, by making an empirical fit of equations to quoted option prices, using only factors that are specifically determinable—stock price P, striking price S, and days to expiration D—and one other factor V, which combines all the other quantities affecting the option price, including the assessment the public places on options at any given time. This factor V is referred to as the *option volatility*. Though it is not strictly a volatility factor, as volatility is usually defined, it does correlate reasonably well with some stock volatility computations. This factor V is determined by working the option price formula backward, solving for V, using actual price data of past options trading. Using this approach, we are able to determine average values that represent normal values. Trends of change in option volatility can be charted, and the relatively undervalued or overvalued

* Fischer Black and Myron Scholes. "Options and Liabilities." *Journal of Political Economy*, **81**, 637 (1973).

† Robert Rebavk. "Risk and Return in CBOE and AMEX Option Trading." *Financial Analysis Journal*, July-August 1975, p. 42.

options can be discovered. The derivation of these formulas is discussed in Chapter 9.

The formulas for computing the normal values of options consist of two components. One gives the time value, which is also the option value for out-of-the-money options. The other component is the intrinsic value, which is added to the time value for in-the-money options and is simply the absolute difference between the stock price and the striking price. The time value T is

$$T = PAVe^{-|P-S|/2PAV} \qquad (2\text{-}1)$$

where P is the stock price, S is the striking price, V is the option volatility, A is a function of the time to expiration, and e is the base of the natural logarithms equal to 2.718. The factor $P - S$, with bars to either side, in the exponent means the absolute value of $P - S$; that is, it is the numerical difference between P and S without regard to algebraic sign. The entire exponent always has a negative sign.

The time value is computed by the same equation whether puts or calls, but because it is proportional to price, an out-of-the-money put has a larger value than a call that is out of the money by the same amount. The time value of an in-the-money put is smaller than that of the corresponding in-the-money call. These values may differ additionally if the put and call volatilities are different. The complete set of formulas is

$$O_c = T \qquad\qquad P < S \qquad (2\text{-}2)$$
$$O_c = T + (P - S) \qquad P > S \qquad (2\text{-}3)$$
$$O_p = T + (S - P) \qquad P < S \qquad (2\text{-}4)$$
$$O_p = T \qquad\qquad P > S \qquad (2\text{-}5)$$

where O_c is the value for calls and O_p is the value for puts. The values of A are given in Appendix C and are a function of the number of calendar days D the option has to go to expiration. It is given by the equation

$$A = (\sqrt{D} + \ln \sqrt{D} + 0.013D - 1) \div 100 \qquad (2\text{-}6)$$

where ln is the natural logarithm.

Although the formulas may be used to compute normal values, an alternative is provided by the tables in Appendix D. To use the formulas directly, one should have a programmable calculator. These are available in small hand-held form and are reasonably priced. Programs for one such calculator are given in Appendix A. We now turn to how options are priced and how these prices vary as various factors change. The charts used for illustration are based on the formulas above.

CALL CHARACTERISTICS

Figure 2–1 illustrates how the value of a typical call option varies with the price of the underlying stock. The curve is drawn for a call at a time of 30 days before expiration having an option volatility V of 0.6, which

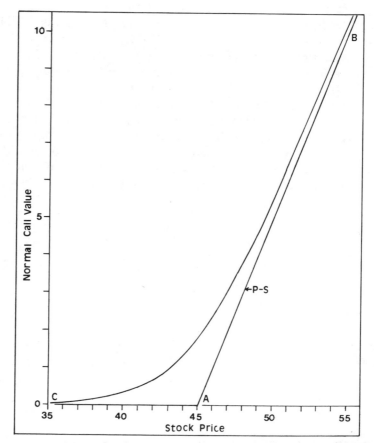

Figure 2–1.   Normal value of a call versus stock price at striking price $S = 45$, having 30 calendar days to expiration, whose option volatility $V = 0.6$.

is about average, and a striking price of 45. When the stock is selling above the striking price, the option should sell for at least as much as the stock is selling above the striking price; otherwise, the call could be exercised, paying the striking price and immediately resold at the higher market price for a small profit, assuming no commissions. There are those who do not pay commissions that watch for such imbalances and enter the market to make a small profit. This is known as *arbitrage*, that is, purchasing in one market for immediate sale in another at a higher price. The straight line AB is the boundary of the lower limit of the call price. It is a plot of $P - S$ versus stock price—P is the stock price and S the striking price—and gives the intrinsic value of in-the-money calls. The call is always priced somewhat higher in this area by the amount of the time value, but, as shown by the chart, the call price approaches this limit, $P - S$, when the stock price moves well above the striking price; that is, the time value approaches zero as the stock price increases far beyond the striking price.

When the stock price is below the striking price, there is no intrinsic value as defined. The call is all time value that approaches zero, or the line AC, as the difference between stock price and striking price becomes large. An option can never have a negative value and, if traded at all, must be for at least one-sixteenth of a point, the minimum increment of pricing.

The time value is a maximum when the stock price is at the striking price; the call price is simply given by the value PAV. Note the call equations both reduce to PAV when $P - S$ (the exponent of e becomes zero so that the exponential factor becomes unity). When this price relationship occurs, the value of V can easily be calculated for the individual stock ($V = $ call price divided by PA).

When the stock price moves away from the striking price by one point in either direction, the option price changes by somewhat less than a point. If the price falls, the call price changes less and less for each point fall in stock price; that is, the slope of the curve decreases. If the stock price rises, the call price increases by a greater amount for each point rise in stock price and approaches a point for point change for very large differences. In this case, the slope of the curve is increasing.

Figure 2–2 shows how the call values depend on the length of time the call has to go before expiration. The option value is naturally greater, the longer it has before expiration. Note that the change in curvature, in the region where $P = S$, becomes more pronounced as the time to expiration decreases.

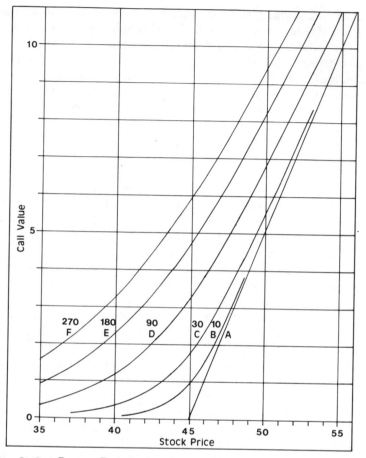

Figure 2–2.   Curves *B* to *F* give the normal value of a call of average volatility (*V* = 0.6) on an underlying stock, at the striking price of 45, as the stock price varies from below to above the striking price. The different curves are for times to expiration ranging from 10 days (curve *B*) to 270 days. Line *A* is a plot of *P* – *S* versus stock price, which is the lower boundary for in-the-money calls. As a call nears expiration, its value approaches this line. Out-of-the-money calls approach the zero axis as they near expiration.

Figure 2–3 shows how the call value varies with stock price for different values of option volatility. Two sets of curves are shown: one for 30 days to expiration and the other for 180 days. Note the greatest curvature in the option curve occurs for the shorter time to expiration and for the low volatility value.

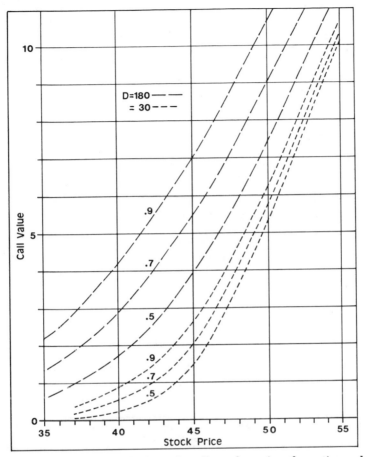

Figure 2–3.   These curves show the effect of varying the option volatility. Two sets are plotted: one for a call near expiration and the other having 180 days to go.

PUT CHARACTERISTICS

The prices of puts move in an opposite direction to prices for calls. When the stock price is below the striking price, the put has an intrinsic value equal to the difference between the stock price and striking price. The plot of $S - P$, shown as line XY in Figure 2–4, is the lower boundary of put values as the stock price falls from the striking price. The put value passes through the point PAV (V is the put volatility) at the point where $P = S$ and then continues decreasing in value as the stock price

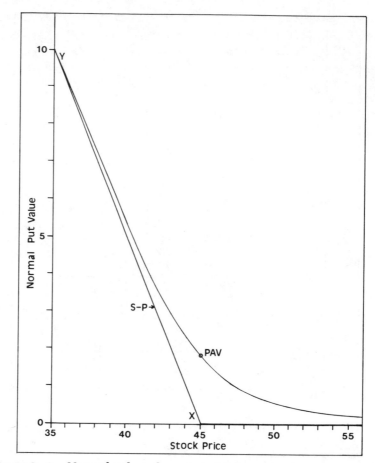

Figure 2–4.   Normal value of a put at striking price $S = 45$, having 30 calendar days to expiration, whose option volatility $V = 0.6$.

increases, approaching the limit of zero for very large values of the stock price. The variation in slope with time to expiration and volatility is the same as for calls, except for the left-to-right reversal.

COMPARISON OF ACTUAL PRICES WITH NORMAL VALUES

We have been careful to point out that the computed normal values are merely reference values and the actual quoted option prices may vary from these values. They should be used merely as guides in making selections and decisions. Lest you get the impression the formulas do a poor job in predicting option prices, we give some illustrations of actual situations. The fact is that the formulas often give rather precise results. The trouble is that you cannot know when any one option may become either overvalued or undervalued or when options as a whole may undergo a change in valuation. Since the formulas were derived by fitting to the average prices over a long period of time, we should expect good results on average, and, for short periods of time, the adjustment of the option volatility V permits good relative comparisons.

A convincing demonstration of how good the fit can be is given in Figure 2–5. Here the closing prices of the April 20 call for Merrill Lynch are plotted versus the closing price of the common stock for the

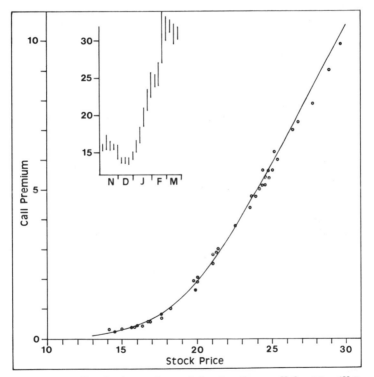

Figure 2–5.   Daily closing prices of the April 20 call for Merrill Lynch are plotted for the time period between December 9, 1975, and March 1, 1976. The price movement was strongly upward during this time, as illustrated by the inset of weekly price ranges. The normal values as calculated by Equations (2–2) and (2–3) are given by the curve for a time 95 days to expiration when the stock price equaled the striking price of 20.

period from December 19, 1975, to March 1, 1976. This example was chosen because Merrill Lynch calls were very actively traded and therefore minimized the possibility of the closing prices of the call and the stock being significantly different in time of execution. Further, for the period of time selected, Merrill Lynch stock advanced rapidly from below the striking price selected to well above. This movement is illustrated by the inset in Figure 2–5 showing the high-low weekly range of the stock price. Also, on this chart, a curve is drawn for the computed values of the call using a value of D, of 95 days, which is the number of

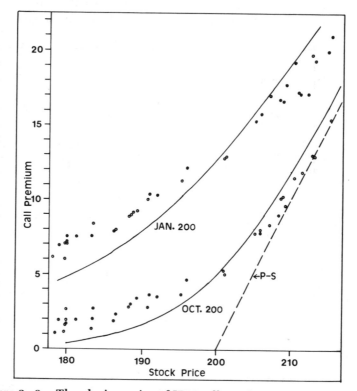

Figure 2–6.   The closing price of IBM calls at the striking price of 200 are plotted for the period from September 5, 1975, to October 31, 1975. The computed normal values are given by the curves for the time to expiration when the stock price crossed 200. The October call had only 18 days to go at this point; so the time value was changing rapidly. This is illustrated by the plotted points being above the curve at the lower prices and falling below the curve at the higher prices, as prices were increasing with time. They reached the $P - S$ boundary line when only a few days of life remained.

days to expiration at the time when the stock price went through the striking price of 20.

At the other extreme in price is the stock of IBM. Its options were also actively traded. Figure 2–6 shows the plotted points for the October and January calls, both at the striking price of 200. The data cover the period from September 5, 1975, to October 31, 1975, except the October call that expired on October 24. For formula comparison, the calculated call values are plotted as solid lines for a time when the stock passed through the striking price of 200. The times to expiration at this point are 18 days for October 200 and 102 days for January 200. The points may appear to have more scatter than for Merrill Lynch, but this is due to a magnification by a factor of 10 (striking price of 200 versus 20 for Merrill Lynch). When considered as a percentage deviation, the results are comparable. The quoted prices of the expiring October 200 call fall away from the computed curve at the higher prices as the time to expiration rapidly approaches. The solid-line curve is for $D = 18$ days. The dashed line (plot of $P - S$) is the lower limit for in-the-money calls. This chart clearly shows how the call price approaches the lower limit of $P - S$ closely during the last several days of option life. The last five plotted points (higher values) are for the last five trading days for this option. Chapter 9 gives additional comparisons between formulas and quoted prices.

OPTION TABLES

You will want to be able to determine normal option values and option volatility for yourself. The most direct method is to use the formulas discussed previously and derived in Chapter 9, but as a practical matter you would need to have at your disposal a programmable calculator. Such calculators are available at a reasonable cost, and a serious options trader would be well advised to purchase one. More will be said later about computer programs. As an alternative, universal option tables have been developed that enable you to read off the desired values for most conditions you encounter in practice.

These tables, in Appendix D, are presented in a unique format that enables you to obtain normal option values as a function of stock price, time to expiration, and option volatility. The values so obtained may not agree precisely with values computed using the formulas, but the difference has no practical significance. The tables enable you to find the normal value for any option on any stock over a range of stock prices for various times to expiration when you know the option volatility. Alternatively you can find the option volatility, using the tables, by using the quoted prices of the option and the stock. Daily closing prices are usually used for this purpose. The tables are constructed so that you may read the values with varying degrees of approximation to the value you would compute, using the formulas, depending on your needs. The explanation of how to use the tables is given in Appendix D.

DETERMINING OPTION VOLATILITY

The tables may be used in a reverse manner to find the option volatility V, using quoted prices for the option and its underlying stock. See the explanation in Appendix D.

When the underlying stock price equals the striking price, the call value is given by the equation $O_c = PAV$; in this case V can be found from the relation $V = O_c/PA$. In fact, we used this relation in establishing the function A by requiring that this function should be such that there is a minimum deviation among the three values of V found by applying this relation to the options expiring at the three times, as established by the option exchanges. See Chapter 9 for a further discussion of this procedure. Of the large number of values used in determining the function A, less than 10% varied significantly from the average, and nearly all of these were found in the value for the option first to expire. When a price pair can be found in which $P = S$, a good value of V can be established by finding the average for the available options. Some care should be exercised in using a value found from an option nearing expiration. This comes about because the small values of the option, as it nears expiration, can vary by a large percentage due to only a fractional change in the option price. The same procedure may be used to find the put volatility factor.

The method above gives good results, but it is not often that you find the underlying stock closing exactly at one of the striking prices. A modification of this technique provides a much wider application. One locates a period in time when the stock price moves through a striking price and plots the quoted option values versus the stock price. A curve is drawn through the average of these plotted points to give a value for the option when the stock price equals the striking price. Refer to Figure 2–1 for the shape of this curve in this region; note that it curves slightly upward. The value of A is selected to correspond to that time when the stock price is near the striking price. Selecting the exact day to establish the value of A in the formula is not critical. The change in the value of A is less rapid as times to expiration are longer. If this is 60

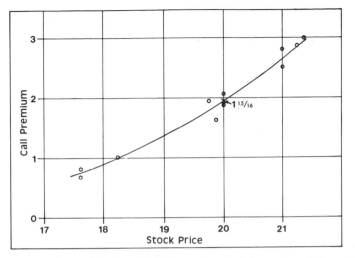

Figure 2–7.   A graphical method is used to find the value of the option, when the stock price equals the striking price, for substitution in the equation V = option value/PA, for determining option volatility. This chart is for Merrill Lynch April 20 call.

calendar days or longer, the difference is less than 5% for a difference of 5 days. More care needs to be used in choosing D for shorter times to expiration. About 10 points, distributed below and above the striking price, are usually sufficient for this plot. This graphical method was used to determine the values of V for use in Figures 2–5 and 2–6. Figure 2–7 shows the plot for the April 20 call of Merrill Lynch during the time of the data plotted in Figure 2–5. The value of D was chosen as the time near the point at which $P = S$, or 95 days.

The values for IBM were determined by plotting points for the January 200 and April 200 calls. The value of V was found to be 0.50 in each case.

One other method is to substitute values of V in the option formulas and compute the option value, changing V until the computed value of the option agrees with the quoted value within the tolerance desired. Values of V to ±0.01 are quite adequate for any practical purpose. This method is practical only if you have a computer, preferably a programmable one.

Best results are obtained when using the options where striking price is near the stock price, and the time to expiration is the greatest. The last two options to expire in exchange-traded options are satisfactory in practice.

The values of V average about 0.6, with 90% falling in the range of about 0.30 to 1.00. A moderately low value may be considered 0.40 and a moderately high value 0.90. The values vary as market conditions vary, and the value associated with each stock varies as the prospect varies for that stock. See Chapter 11 for further discussion of option volatility values.

3 Trading Options

—High leverage
—Selecting the right option

Options may be bought and sold in a trading program in much the same manner as trading a common stock, but there are a few very significant differences. The stock may be considered to have unlimited life, but the option typically exists for a matter of months only. After purchasing a call for trading, you cannot change your mind and decide to become a long-term investor, as with a stock. A stock's price is based on certain values, market conditions, and the public's appraisal of its worth. The option responds directly to the underlying stock price changes but also adds factors of its own. Its premium is further affected by option market conditions, the public's appraisal, and very directly by the remaining life of the option. This time value can work for you or against you.

BUYING CALLS FOR PROFIT

Calls may be bought with the expectation that they will increase in price for a profit, or they may be sold, like selling stock short, if you expect them to decrease in price. In the former, time works against you as the time value of the call decreases bit by bit as it approaches expiration. You may sell a call on the expectation that the underlying stock will fall in price, or you may merely expect to capitalize on the falling price as the time value decreases, hoping to cover at a lower price or even that the call will expire worthless, yielding the entire premium as a profit. In selling calls short, there are margin considerations, but we leave this aspect for later, turning to purchase of calls for appreciation for further discussion.

What should you look for in selecting a call for purchase? You do not look for an undervalued call, hoping it will return to normal or even become overvalued. This may never happen during the life of the call.

You do avoid a significantly overvalued call, for it may return to a normal value and cut your hoped-for gains. The most important factor is to find an underlying stock you expect to increase in price. The call's principal move will be due to the change in stock price. Timing is of utmost importance, and you must understand timing techniques and apply them to the underlying stock to be successful in trading calls. See Chapter 10 for a discussion of short-term timing methods. In general, you can predict the near-term price movements with greater success than the long-term movement of either the market as a whole or a specific stock. Your choice of option expiration date can be matched to the stock timing prediction, but it is desirable to allow some additional time in the option life should the stock take somewhat longer to achieve its objective; that is, do not take a chance on the call's expiring before the stock completes its move. Also, as the call approaches its end of life, the time factor decreases more rapidly and can offset much of the expected gain.

When should you buy a call? Refer to Figure 2–1 and note the shape of the stock-price–call-price curve. You want to buy the call only if it has a chance to increase in price significantly as the stock does. The deep out-of-the-money calls increase in price slowly, particularly when near expiration, but rise faster as the striking price is approached and exceeded to reach the in-the-money condition. Although it is seen that in-the-money calls increase in price more for a point in price increase of the stock, their cost is greater, and the percentage increase grows less and less as the call gets deeper in the money. It is the percentage profit that is important. The following charts illustrate this point.

LEVERAGE

Leverage is a means of magnification. In the stock market *leverage* refers to a situation in which price movements are magnified. Leverage is very important in the option field. For a given percentage change in the price of a stock, its options may change by a much greater amount. This is leverage. We define leverage, when related to the option area, as the ratio of the percentage change in the value of the option to the percentage change in the price of the underlying stock when the stock price changes by a small increment.

Because high leverage is a factor in achieving high option profits, we need to understand how the leverage value is related to the various combinations of option and stock prices. Figure 3–1 illustrates the way leverage varies as the stock price moves from below to above the strik-

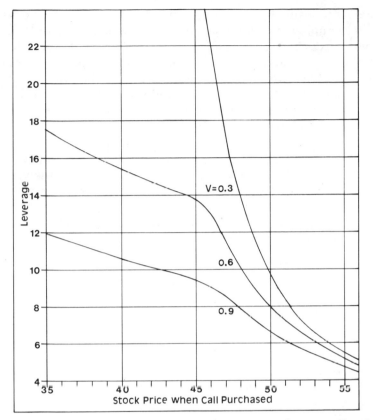

Figure 3–1. These curves show the leverage, or the magnification, achieved in price movement by buying a call instead of the underlying stock for an incremental change in stock price at 30 calendar days before the option expires. The curves are for a striking price of 45. Commissions have not been taken into consideration.

ing price for a typical call. The leverage at each point is computed for a small increment of price movement. If you hold the call for a time during a wide price swing, the leverage changes with stock price, which is illustrated, and also with time (not illustrated here). You may estimate an average for an overall practical value. The important feature to note in Figure 3–1 is that the leverage is greater for out-of-the-money calls and decreases rather rapidly as the call becomes deeper in the money. This tells us something about the striking price we should select for best percentage gains. There is one other important factor that must be considered—commissions. Commissions change the shape of the actual leverage curve, and in particular they greatly reduce the actual leverage for the deep out-of-the-money calls. We take up the effect of commissions later. For the present we continue to look at the leverage curves for other relationships, neglecting, for the time, the effect of commissions. Figure 3–1 shows leverage curves for different values of the volatility. The leverage is higher for the lower volatilities, but this does not necessarily mean that low volatilities are the best buy. The option price movement is very dependent on movement of the stock price. The low volatility implies that the stock may be slower-moving and therefore your gains may be limited.

Figure 3–2 shows how the leverage depends on the time to expiration of a call. The leverage increases as the time to expiration becomes less. We must warn against buying a call too close to expiration to

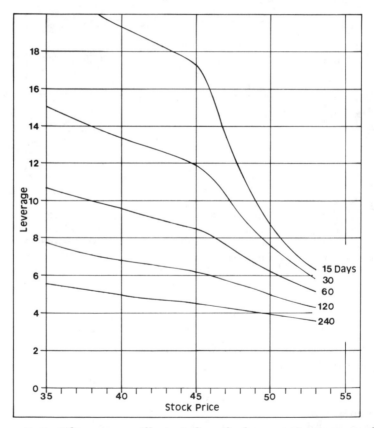

Figure 3–2.   These curves illustrate how the leverage increases as the time to expiration of a call decreases for stock prices around the striking price.

obtain high leverage. At this point the time value is decreasing at a higher rate, and your timing must be better; you may have very little leeway if the stock does not move as expected.

We illustrated how leverage depended on volatility and time to expiration. The third factor, striking price, is different. We saw in Chapter 2 that the formulas for computing call values reduce to $O_c = PAV$ when the stock price equals the striking price. At this point the stock price movement, an increment of P, is magnified by the factor AV to give the incremental movement of O_c. For any given values of A and V this magnification is the same, regardless of the striking price, at $P = S$. Likewise, it may be shown that the leverage is the same for corresponding percentage changes when P is not equal to S. Therefore, when considering price movements on a percentage basis, it does not matter whether you pick a low- or high-priced stock.

COMMISSIONS

We have made our calculations, up to this point, neglecting commission charges; it is simpler, and the answer can be specific. Commissions must not be neglected; they can turn an apparent profit into a loss; they must be fully considered before proceeding on any strategy.

Initially, commission charges were fixed by the CBOE when exchange-traded calls were first introduced. They are no longer fixed and vary somewhat among the different brokerage firms. You will have to check with your own broker to be sure of the rates you will be paying. Most firms follow about the same rates as orginally set up by the CBOE. There are the cut-rate brokers who may or may not appeal to you. They limit their services and generally have minimums per transaction that may not be a reduction in costs if a small trader. In general, the commission schedules are different for options selling under $1.00 and those selling over $1.00. The costs per contract may differ considerably whether you buy or sell one or several contracts on the same option at one time. Some brokers have a minimum commission charge per transaction; therefore you can often save money by trading in multiple contracts—at least two or three at a time—particularly when dealing in medium-priced options.

Some typical rates are as follows: For single options under $1.00, 25% of gross with a minimum of $12.50; 15% of gross plus $1.00 per option; and 6% of gross plus $2.00 per option. For single options over $1.00, most follow the old CBOE schedule of 1.3% of gross plus $12.00 up to $2500 with a minimum of $25.00, or $25.00 plus a surcharge. For larger amounts there are variations. For multiple options over $1.00, it is again 1.3% of gross plus $12.00 plus $6.00 for each option up to ten and then $4.00 for each option above ten, and there may be surcharges of 10 to 15%. You may not find exactly these rates with your broker. They are given here only as typical examples. In order that we may evaluate the effect of commissions, approximate typical charges per option contract (an option on 100 shares of the underlying common stock) are given in Table 3–1, as both a dollar value and a percentage of the contract price. Percentages are rounded, and charges are given to the nearest dollar. This table illustrates the advantage of trading in multiple contracts for certain specific situations. Also, some brokers may have a minimum value per trade, which is higher, that extends this advantage. You can encounter commission charges of as much as 25% one way. If buying a single option for later sale, the commissions could total as much as half of the money involved. You can, in many instances, cut these maximum rates almost in half by trading in two to five or more contracts. When trading two or more options priced at $1.00 to $5.00, a good rule of thumb is to allow three-eighths of a point for round-trip commissions per contract.

The attractive leverages that were illustrated in Figures 3–1 and 3–2 may be wiped out by commission charges if you plan poorly. Figures 3–4 to 3–7 show percentage profits that may be realized when a call is purchased at the plotted stock price if the stock gains 10% and commissions are taken into account. Although we cannot make precise calculations, because commission charges may vary from one situation to another, we can assume an average commission cost based on a sampling of existing charges and illustrate the effect these charges have on possi-

Table 3–1. Approximate Commission Rates for Listed
Options—Values Apply to Each Contract

Option Price	Number of Contracts									
	1		2		3		5		10	
	$	%	$	%	$	%	$	%	$	%
¼	5	20	5	20	5	20	3	11	3	11
½	9	17	9	17	5	10	5	10	5	10
1	25	25	15	12	12	12	10	10	10	10
2	25	13	16	8	14	7	12	6	11	5
3	25	8	18	6	15	5	14	5	12	4
4	25	6	19	5	17	4	15	4	13	3
5	25	5	20	4	18	4	16	3	14	3

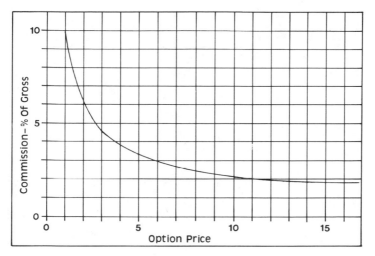

Figure 3–3. Typical commission charges as a percentage of gross price for five option contracts. Actual commissions vary among brokerage firms.

ble profits. Commissions are usually computed by a somewhat complicated formula that produces certain discontinuities at one or more points. For our charts we assume all transactions are in units of five contracts, and we assume a commission of 10% of gross option cost for options priced up to $1.00. For options over $1.00, the commission is assumed to be given as a percentage of cost as read from Figure 3–3.

The curves in Figure 3–4 illustrate the effect of decrease of time value while you wait for the stock price to increase to its objective. The longer you have to wait, the less the profit. The percentage gains are shown for a call of striking price of 45, volatility of 0.70, purchased 60 days before expiration when it takes 10 days (curve A), 20 days (curve B), and 30 days (curve C) for the stock to increase 10% from the plotted price. Average commissions are assumed. The dotted curve represents the upper limit of gain when there is no loss of time value, that is, for an immediate 10% gain in stock price. The maximum gain occurs when the call is purchased at a stock price that is a few points below the striking price. The gains are much lower when the call is deep out of the money because the commissions are high in terms of percentage of the call price. Remember the assumed commissions were for five contracts. If fewer were purchased, the profits would have been even lower. The percentage gains fall rapidly for purchases of calls as they get deeper in the money. This is due to the higher initial cost of the call, with attendant smaller leverage (see Figures 3–1 and 3–2).

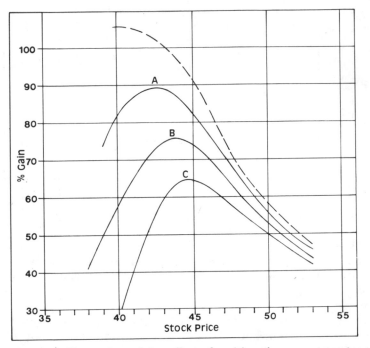

Figure 3–4.   Illustration of the effect of waiting time on percentage of profit: after commissions, for a stock price increase of 10%, and for calls purchased 60 days before expiration. Curves are for a striking price of 45, volatility of 0.7, and commission based on the purchase of five contracts at the plotted stock price. The upper curve, for zero waiting time, is the upper limit of gain.

   The point of maximum gain is seen to move nearer the striking price as the waiting time to achieve the expected gain increases. If purchased too deeply out of the money and the stock moves more slowly than expected, the position could turn into a total loss, as only the intrinsic value, if any, survives at expiration.

   Figure 3–5 is a chart similar to Figure 3–4, but for a range of volatilities, when purchase is made 60 days before expiration and the calls are held 20 days for the stock to gain 10%. The percentage gains are greater, the lower the volatility; this is due to the smaller initial cost of the call, but of course a compensating factor is that the stock may move more slowly for the lower volatility, thus increasing the waiting time, or the stock may not even be expected to make a move as great in magnitude as another stock having a larger volatility.

   Figure 3–6 illustrates possible gain percentages for calls having

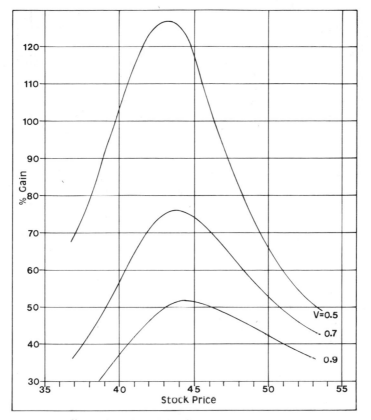

Figure 3–5.   **Effect of option volatility on profits is illustrated. Curves are for calls purchased 60 days before expiration and sold 20 days later, when the stock has increased 10%. The striking price is 45. Commissions are included, based on purchase of five contracts.**

longer times to expiration. All are for a volatility of 0.70. The lower curve is for a call having 240 days to go before expiration and a waiting time of 80 days for the stock price to increase by 10%. The longer waiting time was chosen on the assumption that if you choose a call having this long a life, it is because you expect the stock to take longer to move. Using the same argument, the next curve is for 180 days to go with a waiting time of 60 days, etc. The waiting time is one-third of the time to expiration at time of purchase in each case. One observes the possible gains are much lower as the time to expiration increases.

Even though you expect the stock to make a fast move, the percentage gains are much less if you buy the far-out-to-expire calls, as illus-

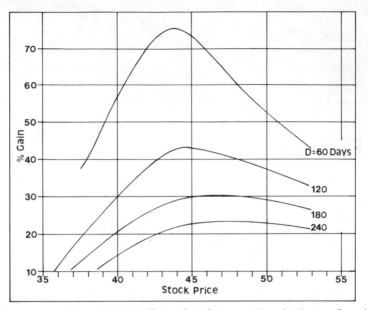

Figure 3–6.   The gain in call profits, for a 10% gain in stock price, decreases as the time to expiration becomes longer. Curves are for a volatility of 0.7, and commissions are included. The waiting time for the stock to gain 10% is one-third of the time to expiration when the purchase is made.

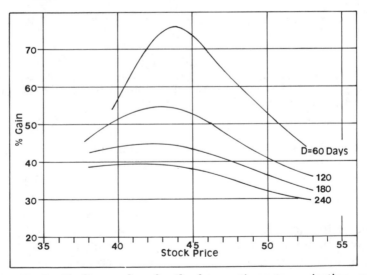

Figure 3–7.   Profits are less for the longer times to expiration, even though the stock achieves its 10% increase in price in 20 days in each case. These curves may be compared with those in Figure 3–6 to see the effect of increased waiting time.

trated by Figure 3–7, in which the waiting time is only 20 days. The gains are not much greater than those shown in Figure 3–6, for the longer waiting times, for the stock to complete its move.

When buying calls for appreciation, not only are the best profits possible by taking a position in calls nearer to expiration, rather than those far out, but the faster movement of the stocks that are suitable for the shorter waiting times permits more turnovers of your cash per year, thus increasing your annualized gains even more.

The important element is how much of a move will the stock make, and this should first be estimated. If it is not great enough, look for another stock. The next element to examine is how fast you expect the stock to move; then select the stock for a good and fast move. Finally, choose the best option of the class for maximizing the gain, but do not play it too close; leave some room for error.

BUYING PUTS FOR PROFIT

If you are bearish and expect the price of a particular stock is going to decline, you can purchase a put with the expectation it will increase in price as the stock falls. Since the normal values for a put follow an inverse relationship to those of a call, buying puts in a falling market is very much like buying a call in a rising market. The put has a time value that decreases as expiration is approached, which works against you—the same as with a call. You likewise need a fast move in stock price to achieve good profits before they are dissipated by a decreasing time value.

Curves for puts may be drawn that are similar to those for calls, except for a reversal of price scale, as illustrated in this chapter. Because the time value is proportional to stock price, there is somewhat of a difference in slope of the put and call option curves. This is illustrated by Figure 3–8, in which the puts are plotted with a reversed price scale for easy comparison. In this figure it is assumed the put and call have the same option volatility V, but this is seldom the case for any particular stock; so the curves would generally be displaced with respect to one another.

RISK

Your risk in trading options on the long side is simply cost of opening the position; you can lose the entire amount. How much risk you are

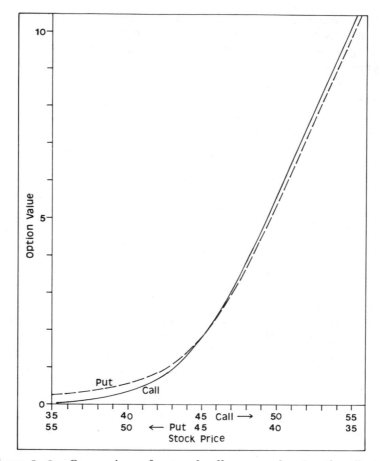

Figure 3–8. Comparison of put and call curves, showing the effect of the inverse stock price relationship.

willing to take should be based on how much you expect to gain should the position work out as planned. Never risk more than you can afford to lose. Do not try to gain everything at once. Commit only a small part of your funds to the possibility of total loss. The gain cannot be so specifically determined as the risk. There will be times when things do not work out. You must plan to gain more than you might lose if you are to come out ahead on average. The oftener you are right, the greater the overall profits. You should search for the best possibilities, act at the best time, and close out quickly the positions that go wrong. Buying options somewhat out of the money, rather than in the money, reduces cost and therefore your risk, and your gains can be as much or more as illustrated by Figures 3–1 to 3–5. Do not crowd the expiration time; allow enough time for the position to work out before the time value runs you into a loss.

PRACTICAL EXAMPLES

Assuming executions at the closing price of the day following a buy or sell signal and typical commission costs, the workout for Alcoa in April 1976 illustrates the advantage of buying out-of-the-money calls. Alcoa gave a buy signal on April 13 and closed the following day at 46½. A sell signal was given April 25, and the stock closed the following day at 52⅛. July calls, having 3 months to go, were available at striking prices of 45 and 50. We can make the following comparison:

In-the-Money Calls

On April 14, buy 2 July 45 calls at 3⅞
   Cost (and risk) = $775 + $37 = $812
On April 26 close position at price of 7⅞
   Received $1575 − $49 = $1526
   Net gain = $714 or 88%

Out-of-the-Money Calls

On April 14, buy 6 July 50 calls at 1¼
   Cost (and risk) = $750 + $64 = $814
On April 26 close position at price of 4
   Received $2400 − $87 = $2313
Net gain = $1499 or 184%

These two situations involve almost identical risks for which trading in the out-of-the-money calls produced a little more than twice the gain. The gain estimates are conservative. You may use this approach in paper trading, and check out your techniques, before taking the plunge into option trading. You may obtain better executions by acting promptly, rather than using a delayed closing price. When following your stock of interest closely, expecting a buy signal, you may act on the signal day before a sizable move is made or at least early the following day. Further, you may sell at a better price if acting prior to the sell signal's actual occurrence when it is obvious the timing is such as to indicate a top area has been reached. See Chapter 10 to learn how to read the buy and sell signals.

Avon gave a buy signal June 1, 1977, and closed the following day at 47½. It gave a sell signal June 22 and closed the next day at 50¾. The workout for 10 July calls is

June 2, buy 10 July 50 calls at ⁷/₈

Cost (and risk) = $875 + $86 = $961

June 23, close position at price of 1⁵/₈

Received $1625 − $102 = $1523
Net gain = $562 or 58%

Pittston had been in a downtrend since July 1976; its minor recovery cycle in June 1977 stalled below the previous high, indicating the purchase of a put. The workout for 5 puts is

July 5, buy 5 August 30 puts at 1½; stock price 28⁵/₈

Cost (and risk) $750 + $57 = $807

August 19, close position at price of 5; stock price 24⁷/₈

Received $2500 − $82 = $2418
Net gain = $1611 or 200%

Santa Fe International, in an uptrend for many months, was highly favorable for call purchases but also exhibited marked downside reactions in a cyclic pattern. Puts and calls could have been purchased alternately when puts started trading. For example,

June 2, 1977, stock price 50¾; buy 3 July 50 calls at 2¹¹/₁₆

Cost (and risk) = $806 + $45 = $851

July 1, stock price 55⅛; close position at 5

Received $1500 − $55 = $1445
Net gain = $594 or 70%

Buy 3 October 55 puts at 2⁷/₈

Cost (and risk) = $863 + $45 = $908

August 5, stock price 51½; close position at 4½

Received $1350 − $52 = $1298
Net gain = $390 or 43%

The general market weakness at this time made it advisable to defer further purchase of calls.

PUTTING IT ALL TOGETHER

The strategy of buying options for appreciation is one of the simplest and most straightforward techniques you can use in trading in options. It provides great leverage but at the same time runs a risk of total loss of your committed funds.

Chapter 2 discussed normal values of any option of interest. This normal value can be referred to a long-time or short-time average by finding the average value of V that applies to the time desired. You may even compare the different calls of a given stock on a daily basis to determine their relative under- or overvaluations.

If you are to maximize your chances of success, there are several conditions that should prevail. First, you should go with the general market, buying calls in a rising market, puts in a falling market. You can, at times, find individual stocks that are making strong moves against the market averages, but going with the market you have a broader selection. Even in a strong bull or bear market there are usually short trading cycles of a few weeks' duration. You should operate in phase with these minor movements. See Chapter 10 for a discussion of timing techniques. If you want to learn more about market cycles and their prediction, see references 1 and 2, Appendix E.

Having favorable market conditions, you are ready to select promising stocks. For this you need high-low weekly bar charts of a large group of stocks or a specialized group covering stocks on which options are traded. It is impractical to try to maintain your own plots of the large number that may be desired, since they can be purchased quite reasonably on a monthly issue basis. These charts provide you with the data needed to select several stocks that show desired characteristics. They have a good intermediate trend, dependable cyclic movements, and good price swings. Next, you need a daily high-low chart of your selected favorable stocks, and it is well to make these charts yourself. The number involved need not be so great as to be a burden to maintain. You may also desire to plot the closing price of one or two selected options on these stock charts. Doing your own plotting keeps the chart right up to the day, and you will at times need this information, for the options you will want to buy are at least expected to move fast if you have made a good selection. There are chart services giving daily plots and published weekly; you can use these and add to those of interest during the week. Doing your own is more than cutting expenses; you gain a better feel for the market movement as a whole and how individual stocks behave. You need enough history on these daily charts to show up the trading cycles and trend lines in order to establish the buy and sell signals of the individual stock and to permit estimates of price objectives.

Having found a promising stock, you now look at the available options. First, they should be actively traded, and, second, they should have enough life remaining for the stock to make its objective before they approach expiration. We have already devoted considerable discussion to the price movement of options relative to the stock price around the striking price, and charts we have discussed point out the advantages of buying options that are somewhat out of the money. At this point you may need to do a little calculation to pick that stock whose option stands to produce the greatest percentage gain, taking into consideration the separation between stock price and striking price, whether it is desirable to delay a little for a greater certainty as to the price movement, and which stock or stocks are the best selection. A final check on the normal value of the option should be made; then place your order at a limit so as not to pay for an excessively overvalued option.

Selling is much simpler but more difficult. This may sound like a contradiction. First, you do not have the selection process to go through, only one decision—to hold or sell—but this decision is made very difficult for most people because of the psychological factor that is introduced. You must learn to overcome this barrier to doing the correct thing. You determine your objectives before opening the position, and you had better stick with them and act accordingly or be sure that any change you make is arrived at by as objective an analysis as when you made the buy selection. Do not hold on for a little more profit, trying to pick the exact maximum. Your sell signal invariably comes on a reversal in price; do not wait for the price to return to its value a few days earlier. It is better to try to pick the sell area and sell before the actual signal occurs. When the price movement goes against you, cut your losses promptly.

ROLLOVER

When you are fortunate enough to own a call on a stock that is going "straight up," it is not always desirable to hold this call, even though its value is continually increasing. Rather, you may be able to make more money by selling the call when it gets somewhat in the money and purchase a call at a higher striking price and somewhat out of the money, thus rolling over your commitment. You have several possibilities: you can maintain the same number of calls, pocketing profits as they arise; you can take out your original cost and trade on the profits only; or you can recommit both your cost and profits in as many contracts as they will buy. Rolling over can be profitable under proper circumstances, even though you pay more commissions in the process. For example, had you been interested in Merrill Lynch calls during the period of time covered in Figure 2–5, you might have bought 2 April 20 calls on January 9, 1976, at $7/16$ for a total cost of $103, including commissions. If these were held to March 1, 1976, they were worth $12 7/8$ (closing price), and if sold at this price would have netted $2409 profit after commissions.

Alternatively, you might have rolled over the April 20s on January 30, selling at $4 3/8$ and buying April 25s at $1 7/8$ when the common closed at $23 1/2$. If these were held to March 1 and the position closed out at 8, the results would have been as follows, including typical commissions:

	Debit	Credit
January 9, buy 2 April 20 calls at $7/16$	$103	
January 30, sell 2 April 20 calls at $4 3/8$		$ 836
buy 4 April 25 calls at $1 7/8$	800	
March 1, close position at 8		3115
Net profit = $3048		

Your profit was over $600 greater than if you held the original calls. A striking price of 30 was not offered in the April series, and it was not available in the July series until February 24 at a price of $3 7/8$. It was more profitable to hold the April calls than to roll over into the July series if planning to close out on March 1.

4 Short Side of the Options Game

—Short sellers have an "option"

In the previous chapter we discussed purchasing calls with the expectation that the stock would increase in price and the call could be sold later at a profit. Also, we discussed buying puts when we expect the stock to fall in price, making the put more valuable, which could then be sold at a profit. In both of these situations we are operating on the long side of the options market. In each, the decision is yours as to what to do with your holding. Your loss can be no more than your purchase cost plus the commission.

WRITING OPTIONS

There is the other side of the coin; you can sell an option as your opening transaction. This is much like short selling of a stock, but there are some interesting and important differences. When selling a stock, you must borrow the stock certificate (your broker takes care of this). This is not necessary with options. An option is merely a contract and does not represent a physical asset, as in the case of a stock. The Options Clearing Corporation supplies the other party to the contract by becoming the buyer.

Another important difference is that options have a short life but stocks are normally a permanent asset. Although you must give continued attention to your short position in stocks, time does not terminate this position. With options you must take further action within a limited time period, or action will be taken for you. You must also face the possibility that the action may be taken by the other party to the contract when shorting options. You do not have complete control of your situation. Any action you may desire to take must be before the option is exercised or expires.

WRITING CALLS

When you open a position by selling a call, you make a contract to deliver a stock at a specified price if the other party to your contract chooses to exercise his privilege. There are two quite different situations in which you may find yourself if the call is exercised. If you owned the stock when you sold the call, you are said to be covered; that is, if the call is exercised, you can deliver the stock you own. In this case you can determine your risk at the time you sell the call, for you know exactly what price you would receive for the stock (striking price) and you can calculate the commission involved. Whether you make an overall profit depends on what you paid for the stock. Selling a call on your stock is often referred to as *writing a call*, and this is known as *covered writing*.

You may sell a call without owning the stock. This is known as *uncovered writing*, or writing a *naked* call. In this case, you are running the risk of having to purchase the stock at the market for delivery to the caller if he chooses to exercise his contract. The stock could have gone up any amount, and your possible loss is unlimited. You also have to pay two commissions: one to purchase the stock and another for the immediate sale to the call holder. Many brokerage houses give a discount for short turnaround situations such as this. Further, you have to supply margin; so additional funds or marginable securities must be provided. Margin is discussed later.

Covered writing has an element of risk, which is often overlooked. When you write a call on a stock you own, you must retain this stock as long as you have the position in the call. Your stock could go down, and you might want to sell before it goes down further. If you do sell, you become an uncovered writer, and margin must be supplied. You can of course close your call position by a purchase when selling your stock. The premium you received when the call was sold gives you protection on the downside to the extent of the proceeds from the sale, but this may not be sufficient to warrant holding your position. You may choose to eliminate your entire position with respect to this stock.

WRITING PUTS

If you sell a put, you contract to take stock from the buyer of the put if he chooses to exercise his privilege. The price is fixed (striking price); so you know exactly what your situation may be. You may want the stock at this price anyway, and selling a put may allow you to obtain it at a price less than present market price. You must be prepared to make the purchase at any time; so the funds required must be available in a liquid form and should be such as not to force you to sell something at a loss unless you so desire.

Selling puts is uncovered writing, but you may also sell short the underlying stock at the same time, or you could already be short the stock. In this case, if the put is exercised, the stock you are forced to buy covers your short position, and you can calculate exactly what your risk is. All the features of selling stock short apply, such as paying the dividend.

CLOSING SHORT POSITIONS

The majority of options are not exercised until near the expiration date, but you cannot depend on this for the specific option you have sold. If it has not been exercised, you can close your position by purchasing an identical option in a closing transaction. This is frequently done to collect profits when the stock has moved as expected. When the option has decreased to a small value, you have accrued most of your possible profit, and it may be better to close the position and look elsewhere for the action. The alternative is merely to hold on with the expectation that the option will expire worthless, but you are running a risk of the stock price's reversing and losing the profit available for the taking.

We saw in the previous chapter that when purchasing an option for appreciation, time works against you; that is, if nothing else changes, the value of the option decreases with time. If selling an option short with the expectation of later covering at a lower price, time is with you. You stand to gain, both because the stock price moves in the desired direction and because the time value of the option decreases. For both puts and calls, time is with you when selling short and against you on the long side.

Selling calls and selling puts differ in the following respect. The price of a call increases as the stock price increases above the striking price without limit. The price of a put increases as the stock price decreases, but since the stock cannot decrease below zero, there is a limit to the rise in price of the put. In other words, the potential for gain of in-the-money puts diminishes as the stock price falls, and the put sells at intrinsic value earlier, relative to expiration time, than in-the-money calls. This leads to more early exercises in puts than in calls. If planning to close a short position in puts, you should be concerned about early exercise.

5 Margin

—You have to cover your risk

When you buy a security, you may pay for it with cash, but if your credit is good enough, you may establish an account with your broker in which you need only to pay a certain percentage in cash, the remaining being loaned to you by your broker. You will be charged interest on this loan at a rate that varies with the money interest rates and may be changed from time to time. You do not have a fixed interest rate agreement, as with an ordinary note.

The Federal Reserve Board establishes how much can be loaned to you for the purchase of stock. If this is 40% of the cost of the stock, you have to put up the remaining 60% in cash, which is known as the customer's *margin*. Special accounts set up with your broker to permit you to borrow a part of the costs of your stock purchases are known as *margin accounts*.

REGULATIONS

The federal government, through the Federal Reserve Board, controls the amount of credit any lending institution is allowed to extend for the purchase of securities. Regulation T applies to broker-dealer firms. Other regulations apply to banks and other types of lenders. Regulation X makes you, the borrower, just as responsible as the lender for adhering to the rules.

If the Board believes an excessive amount of credit is being extended for purchase of securities, it may raise the margin requirement. It was as high as 90% during 1959. If they feel the credit is being unnecessarily restrained, they can lower the requirement. It has never been below 50% in recent years. The Board typically allows greater credit for purchase of bonds, but we are interested only in stocks and options and so will not go further into this aspect.

Even though you may always desire to put up cash for all your transactions, thus never borrowing from your broker and consequently never being charged interest, if you participate in the wide variety of option strategies, you will have to abide by certain margin requirements. Though your broker will inform you on the details, you need to understand the broad aspects in order to know just what your commitment is.

Although the minimum margin requirements are established by the Federal Reserve Board, additional requirements may be imposed by the various exchanges and further by your individual broker. Before you start, find out what your broker requires. The discussion that follows describes typical situations that will guide you in further discussions with your broker.

MARGIN SECURITIES

Securities registered on a national securities exchange can be used as collateral for a loan to purchase securities to the extent permitted by regulation. In addition, certain over-the-counter (OTC) stocks, as determined by the Board, are also subject to margin regulation. A list is periodically published by the Board.

Under present regulations, options have no loan value in a margin account.

MARGIN AND EQUITY

Two conditions must be met if you are operating under margin conditions that are the combined result of margin requirements of the Federal Reserve Board, the stock exchanges, and your individual brokerage house. One is an equity requirement. This can be met by your stock and bond holdings in your account or cash. You should not trade in options on more than a fraction of your capital; so ordinarily the equity requirement will be met by your holdings, you can merely let your broker keep the books, and it will cost you nothing. The other is the margin requirement that always arises when you have a short position. This can sometimes be met in whole or in part by offsetting long positions if they will completely cover the short risk; even then, some brokers may require a minimum margin, in addition to a minimum equity. Any uncovered risk must be covered by a margin that is equivalent to cash;

that is, it must be either cash supplied by you in your account or securities in your account that can be turned into cash by your broker if needed to cover the short position.

The regulations may change after you have taken a postion. You must be prepared to meet any changes should they occur. Also, changes in prices may call for more margin; you get a *margin call*.

MARGIN AS APPLIED TO OPTIONS

Margin regulations change from time to time; so check out the situation with your broker before entering into option transactions. Currently the margin requirements are broadly as follows.

The purchase of a call or put must be paid for in cash at the time of the transaction. The cash thus must be on hand in your account. Such purchases may be made in a special cash account, and if this is the extent of your option activity, you may not have to establish a margin account.

If you are writing a call or put, you may be required to open a margin account. If you write a call on stock you own, you do not need to supply margin. If you write a put, you must have cash available to purchase the stock if the put is exercised. The stock can, of course, be purchased on margin; so you have to put up the cash only beyond the loan value of the stock, but you will pay interest on the loan.

The margin requirements are established in such a manner as to ensure you can keep your commitment no matter what happens. The initial requirement is set up when you first enter the transaction. If the situation changes, you may be required to supply additional margin to bring you back to a safe credit risk. This second requirement is known as the *maintenance requirement*. This can get pretty complicated, but your broker will keep you advised as changes occur.

Writing Covered Calls. Assuming a 55% margin requirement, if you purchase 100 shares of a stock and simultaneously sell a call contract, the funds required are 55% of the cost of the stock minus the funds received from the sale of the call. As an example, suppose the stock price is 30 and you received $450 for the call. The stock costs $3000, and you need to put up 55% of this, or $1650, but the $450 received for the call is applied to reduce the amount of cash required to $1200. You could then own the stock for $1200 in cash plus a loan of $1350 on which you pay interest. Alternatively you could put up $2550 in cash, and there would be no interest charges. Of course commission charges must be added.

Writing Calls Naked. Presently, Regulation T requires a margin of 30% of the market price of the stock—some brokers may require more—minus the amount received for the call plus or minus the amount the call is in or out of the money. As an example, if the stock price is 32 and the call with a striking price of 30 sold for $500, you would have to put up 30% of $3200 equal to $960 minus $500 (what you receive for the call) plus $200 (difference between stock price and striking price of the call), or a total of $660. If the stock continues to rise above the striking price, additional margin will be required.

There are other requirements that may come into the picture when operating on the short side of the market. One is a minimum margin of $250 for each uncovered call contract. Another is the minimum equity requirement in your account that is required for you to participate on the short side. This will be brought out when you establish your margin account. A minimum equity is required in the various short positions discussed below.

Selling Puts. You may sell a put without a position in the underlying stock. If you do, you must be prepared to purchase the stock at any time during the life of the put if it should be exercised. This situation establishes a margin requirement that in general parallels that for calls. As an example, for a stock selling at 32, assume a put with striking price of 30 is selling at 2½; then the margin for selling a naked put would be 30% of the value of the stock equal to $960 minus $250 (what you received for the put) minus $200 (the out-of-the-money difference), or a total of $510. Note, in this case, the put is out of the money but the call was in the money. If you own the underlying stock, this makes no difference.

If you are short the underlying stock or sell it short simultaneously with the sale of the put, the margin required for the short sale standing alone must be met, and there is no further requirement on selling the put. This corresponds to the covered writing of calls.

Options as Margins. In the more complex strategies that are discussed later, a long option position may sometimes be used to meet in whole or in part the margin requirement for a short option position. The margin on an option sold naked can be met by the purchase of an option of the same class at the same striking price but expiring at a later date. The money received for the short option can be applied to the cost of the long option with the remainder in cash to meet the requirement that an option must be fully paid for at the time of purchase.

Also, the margin on a call sold naked can be met by the purchase of a call expiring at the same or later date having a striking price lower than the striking price of the naked call. Likewise, if you sell a put, the margin can be met by the purchase of a put expiring at the same time or a later date having a striking price higher than the striking price of the put sold.

If instead you purchase a call at a striking price higher than the call sold naked, expiring on the same or later date, you will have a margin requirement equal to the difference in striking prices. Similarly, if you purchase a put at a striking price lower than the put sold short, expiring on the same or later date, you will have a margin requirement equal to the difference in striking prices. Alternatively, you may compute the margin on the naked option alone and choose the lesser value.

6 Option Spreading

—Reduce your risk
—Make time your ally

An *option spread* is established by a sale of one option and a purchase of a different option of the same type on the same underlying stock. There are two basic varieties and several variations. One, the *horizontal, calendar,* or *time spread* is the sale of one option at a given striking price and the purchase of another option of the same type at the same striking price with a different expiration date. The other is the *vertical* or *striking price spread*, in which both the long and short positions expire on the same date, but the long and short positions are taken at different striking prices. There are variations and combinations of these two basic forms. We now examine the various spread strategies. Often spread strategies are discussed on a simplified basis, assuming your position will work out ideally and neglecting commissions. These can look very impressive, but the ideal situation seldom develops, and commissions are always with you. Your anticipated gains must take these considerations into account. You must understand how spread values vary with the various parameters in order to time your transactions properly. This chapter develops aids for evaluating spreads.

BALANCED HORIZONTAL CALL SPREADS

This section is concerned with call options. The ordinary horizontal spread is to sell one option and buy another in the same stock at the same striking price but expiring at a later time. In the standarized exchange-traded options the time separation may be 3 or 6 months. The first option to expire may have less than 3 months to expiration but could also be farther down the line. This type of spread is entered into with the expectation that the dollar difference required to open the position will be less than the dollar spread at some later time, when the position can be closed to produce an overall profit. You depend on time, which works in your favor, to increase the spread differential. The time value of the call you sold decreases at a more rapid rate, because it is nearer expiration, than the call you buy. Since the purchase, or long position, has a larger time value than the earlier to expire, or short position, it costs you the spread difference plus commissions, but this may be considerably less than merely taking a long position. For maximum profit, one hopes that the short call will expire worthless and the amount that was collected on its sale will be all profit. The long call will have some value that will be greater, the higher the stock price; but the stock price must not exceed the striking price if the short call is to expire worthless. One usually plans to maintain the position until the near call expires, but it may be desirable to close the position by buying the nearer-term call and selling the long one at some earlier time if the price relations are advantageous.

Tax treatment of options has been changed in recent years. Some previously available tax advantages are no longer available. The Tax Reform Act of 1976 made options a capital asset whether a purchase or sale. Other changes have eliminated the availability of favorable treatment for longer holding times in so far as exchange-traded options are concerned. Since tax laws can be changed at any time, you should keep abreast of the changes that affect your trading and investing in securities. Brokerage houses and security exchanges frequently distribute pamphlets summarizing such changes.

Margin can increase your capital requirement. The margin requirements may vary from time to time and from broker to broker; so you should check the current requirements. Since in the normal horizontal spread you are long a more distant to expire option for each option sold short, the normal margin is met as long as the spread position is maintained. There have been times when some brokers required a minimum margin for each spread contract.

There are various ways for you to establish the spread position. You may place an opening spread order with your broker by merely specifying the debit difference between the two options. Only the difference determines the net cost before commissions. This avoids specifying the two prices precisely in order to establish the initial cash outlay. The two option prices move up and down together; so you can achieve your initial position even though the options are moving rapidly. For example, the closing prices for the Homestake Mining class of calls, together with the spread differential, are given in Table 6–1. Note the April and July calls, with about 3 and 6 months to expiration. You could expect to be able to open a position at the striking level of 30 for about 1¼ point

Table 6–1. Closing Stock and Call Prices for Homestake Mining for the Week of January 10, 1977, for Three Striking Prices and the Corresponding Spread Values

Date	Stock Price	Option	Price	Option	Price	Spread
1-10-77	35 1/4	Apr 30	6 1/8	July 30	7 1/4	1 1/8
1-11-77	35 5/8		6 3/8		7 3/8	1
1-12-77	35 5/8		6 5/8		7 7/8	1 1/4
1-13-77	35 5/8		6 1/8		7 3/4	1 5/8
1-14-77	35 5/8		6		7 1/4	1 1/4
1-10-77	35 1/4	Apr 35	2 5/8	July 35	3 3/4	1 1/8
1-11-77	35 5/8		2 7/8		3 3/4	7/8
1-12-77	35 5/8		2 15/16		3 3/4	13/16
1-13-77	35 5/8		3		4 1/4	1 1/4
1-14-77	35 5/8		2 7/8		4	1 1/8
1-10-77	35 1/4	Apr 40	7/8	July 40	1 3/4	7/8
1-11-77	35 5/8		1		1 3/4	3/4
1-12-77	35 5/8		15/16		1 15/16	1
1-13-77	35 5/8		1		2	1
1-14-77	35 5/8		15/16		1 15/16	1

spread, at the 35 striking price for about 1⅛ point spread, and at the 40 level for about 1 point spread. You may have difficulty getting an execution at a specified debit if it is too close. Both the purchase and sale have to be available at the price differential or better.

You can, of course, set up the spread position one leg at a time. Referring again to Homestake Mining, for the week shown, in which the common price was stable, you might have been able to sell the April 40 call for as much as 1 and buy the July 40 call for as little as 1¾, resulting in only ¾ point spread. If the stock is in a predictable trend, you might be able to establish one leg at a time without any differential or even for a profit. If you execute the long side first, you will have to put up the full purchase price in cash, which will be tied up until the sell is executed. If you execute the short side first, you will have to put up the margin required, for selling naked calls, until the spread is completed.

With respect to setting up one leg at a time, if your timing is poor, you could be trapped if the stock moved in the wrong direction, and the reduced risk you hoped to achieve by using a spread would be lost. If you are so sure of the price movement as to feel safe in setting up one leg at a time, you must question the wisdom of entering a spread position rather than a purchase or sale, as may be indicated, which would produce a greater profit.

The spread may be closed by buying in a closing transaction the first to expire option and selling your long position, you may have both sides of the spread executed at the same time at a specified credit difference, or you may close one leg at a time. If you hold the position until the first call expires and the stock price is less than the striking price, this call will be worthless, leaving you with a long call that will have some value. You may continue to hold it or close it out.

When evaluating the possible gains in the spread, commissions are very important. They can contribute a significant amount to the cost of opening a spread. Setting up multiple spreads usually reduces the effect of the commission. Generally, two spreads make a major reduction in commission cost per spread, and dealing in greater numbers makes some further reduction.

Assume you established a spread position in Homestake Mining options in January 1977 by selling two April 40 calls at $^{15}/_{16}$ and buying two July 40 calls at $1^{15}/_{16}$ for 1 point differential. Using typical commissions, your total cost would be about $250. The last trading day for the April options was Friday, April 15, 1977. Thursday the 14th Homestake closed at $40^5/_8$, and you would have to buy back the April options to avoid their being exercised if they had not been exercised at some earlier date. The closing prices on the 15th were $^1/_8$ for the April option and $2^9/_{16}$ for the July option. Assume the position is closed out at these prices; then your credit amounts to $448, which results in a $198 profit on a $250 cash outlay. As it worked out, you would have made about the optimum profit.

If you had chosen the striking price of 35 and opened the position by selling two April 35 calls at $2^7/_8$ and buying two July calls at 4, your risk would be about $298. If you held until the April calls expired, the April call traded at $5^1/_4$ and the July at $5^3/_4$, and your loss would be $282. If you had opened this spread, it should have been on the assumption that Homestake was to remain at a price of about 35 for the next 3 months. As the stock price moved up, you should close out your position and take your loss, which could be not much more than the four commissions if you do not wait too long. We now explore these points in more detail.

Table 6–2 lists the closing prices for a number of calls with the spread as of October 20, 1975. The spread for these calls is given in the last column of this table as of 1 day before the January calls expired. Had you entered into a spread in any of this list, most would have shown a loss, and the few that would yield a profit would have given minimal results. All this in spite of the unusually sharp rise in stock prices during January. This illustrates that there is more to making

Table 6–2. Closing Prices and Spreads—as of 10/20/75 and 1/15/76

These stocks had January and April calls for a striking price somewhat above the stock price on October 20, 1975, and would have been candidates for a time spread purchase. The last column gives the spread values as of January 15, 1976, the day before the January calls expire.

Stock	Stock Price	Striking Price	January Call Price	April Call Price	Spread 10-20-75	Spread 1-15-76
Avon	42	50	$1^5/_{16}$	$2^5/_{16}$	1	$^3/_8$
Beth S	$36^1/_2$	40	1	$1^7/_8$	$^7/_8$	$^{13}/_{16}$
Bruns	$9^5/_8$	15	$^3/_{16}$	$^3/_8$	$^3/_{16}$	$^5/_{16}$
Citicp	$29^5/_8$	40	$^1/_4$	$^3/_4$	$^1/_2$	$^1/_8$
Delta	$32^5/_8$	40	$^5/_8$	$1^3/_{16}$	$^9/_{16}$	$1^{15}/_{16}$
FNM	$15^1/_2$	20	$^1/_4$	$^5/_8$	$^3/_8$	$^3/_{16}$
Halbtn	145	180	$1^1/_2$	$3^1/_2$	2	$1^5/_8$
Homstk	$40^1/_2$	50	1	$2^1/_4$	$1^1/_4$	$^1/_4$
IBM	$211^1/_2$	220	$8^7/_8$	$13^7/_8$	5	$2^7/_8$
INA	$34^1/_8$	40	$^5/_8$	1	$^3/_8$	$1^1/_4$
ITT	$20^3/_4$	25	$^3/_8$	$^3/_4$	$^3/_8$	$^{15}/_{16}$
In Har	23	30	$^3/_{16}$	$^9/_{16}$	$^3/_8$	$^1/_4$
In Min	39	45	$1^5/_{16}$	$2^3/_8$	$1^1/_{16}$	$^7/_{16}$
Kenn C	$29^1/_2$	40	$^3/_{16}$	$^{13}/_{16}$	$^5/_8$	$^1/_4$
Kresge	$33^1/_4$	35	$1^{13}/_{16}$	$2^{13}/_{16}$	1	$1^{11}/_{16}$
Loews	$21^1/_8$	25	$^9/_{16}$	$1^1/_{16}$	$^1/_2$	$1^3/_{16}$
MMM	$58^1/_4$	60	$3^3/_8$	$4^3/_4$	$1^3/_8$	$2^1/_2$
Mc Don	$52^3/_8$	60	$2^1/_8$	$3^1/_2$	$1^3/_8$	$2^{13}/_{16}$
Pennz	$21^3/_8$	25	$^7/_{16}$	$^3/_4$	$^5/_{16}$	$^3/_{16}$
Tesoro	$14^1/_2$	20	$^5/_{16}$	$^5/_8$	$^5/_{16}$	$^3/_{16}$
Tex In	$100^5/_8$	120	$2^1/_2$	$4^1/_8$	$1^5/_8$	$2^1/_4$

profits in options than just buying horizontal spreads. Let us examine the normal values as provided by the option formulas, Equations (2–2) and (2–3).

Figure 6–1 shows computed spread differences in the vicinity of the striking price of 45 at different times to expiration for calls separated by 90 days in time to expiration. The upper curve, designated 0/90 represents the spread value at the time the near-term short call expires. It is a maximum when the stock price is equal to the striking price. For prices less than this value, the spread is just equal to the value of the long call. For prices above the striking price, the value of the long call is reduced by the value of the short call, which at this point in time is exactly equal to the difference between the stock price and the striking price.

Other curves in this figure give spread values for times when both calls have some time to go. These curves show that the spread values

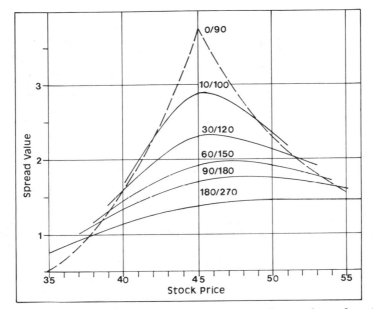

Figure 6–1. Values of the balanced horizontal call spread as a function of stock price for various times to expiration of the short call when the long call has 90 additional days to go. The striking price is 45, and option volatility 0.7. Commissions are not included.

are less for longer times to expiration, but the difference is relatively small when the stock price is well below the striking price. Realizing that to make the greatest profit, it is desirable to hold the spread position until the nearest-term call expires and that the stock should be near the striking price, the near-term call should not be too far from expiration when opening the spread. The small added cost of opening the spread is offset by the better predictability of price movement over the near term than for a time more months in the future. Even though the absolute gain may be less, if the spread is opened with only a month or two to go, you can perhaps initiate a second or even a third spread in the time you would be waiting for a long-term spread to mature. This indicates that a good strategy is to look for a stock whose price movement is in a good predictable cycle, which is expected to top out at a price near one of the available striking prices, at a time of an option expiration date; then open the spread near the bottom of the cycle. One should not consider situations in which the expected price increase is less than about 10%. These limitations of price and time restrict the possibilities of finding good horizontal spreads at any given time but are necessary to achieve success.

The chart demonstrates you can be either bullish or bearish when using the time spread. If bullish, you choose a striking price at which the calls are out of the money with the expectation that the stock price will rise to the striking price. For best profits, you need to predict not only that the stock will go up in price but that it will go up at such a rate as to reach the striking price close to the time the near-term call expires. If you allow the price to get too far above the striking price before closing out the spread, you will probably suffer a loss. If this appears likely to happen, you should close the position not far above the striking price, since the spread has the maximum credit difference in this region. Even though the curves are relatively flat near their maximums, as the price goes up, commissions to close the position increase; so you should not delay.

If, instead the stock goes down in price, you may at some point want to sell your long call and let the short call ride. Such action will call forth a margin requirement to carry the short position. If the stock does nothing, you can hold on until the short call expires and sell your long call, which will have some value, but an examination of the curves shows it will not be worth much more than the cost of opening the spread if the spread was fairly deep out of the money. When commissions are paid, you may expect to have an overall loss.

If you are bearish, you could open the spread when in the money and hold for the stock to fall in price. The curves show a higher opening spread cost than for the bullish position, and further, commissions will be larger. Bearish horizontal call spreads are therefore somewhat unattractive.

Another situation is one in which you expect the stock price not to vary over a considerable period of time. The curves show that if you open the spread near the striking price, when the calls have several months to expiration, the spread credit value will increase as time passes. In fact, you might expect a twofold increase. This could be profitable even after the total of four commissions you might have to pay. The critical aspect is that you have to catch the stock near the striking price some time near the expiration of the short call. An undesirable feature is that this strategy requires considerable time to work out; so the turnover of your funds is limited and thus annualized profits reduced.

All in all, trading in time spreads is a tricky business. Although risks can be small, possible gains are likewise pretty limited, and things must go right for you to come out ahead. There may be times when the calls deviate from their normal values that can give you an added advantage. Spotting these situations is not easy. You almost have to determine the normal values for the two calls involved, but we have illustrated where in time and stock price you should look; so this reduces the task.

We have shown in Figure 6–1 the situation for one striking price (45) and one volatility (0.70). Referring to the formulas for computing normal values of calls, we see that when the stock price is at the striking price, the value of the call is given by PAV. This locates a point on the curve near the maximum. Since the value is directly proportional to the volatility V, the spread values will be proportional to V, or the spreads will be smaller for low volatilities and larger for the high volatilities. Thus you will find spreads ranging from a fraction of a point to several points if you examine the closing price quotations. In the same manner, the call values are directly proportional to the stock price; so again the spread values will vary over a wide range as you go from low-priced to high-priced stocks. It is these characteristics which make it difficult to pick a good horizontal spread from the price quotations.

There is one aid to spotting abnormal spread situations. Refer to Figure 6–1. You will note that the spread values around the striking price are relatively flat for the far out in time spreads. Further, the two lower curves give values for two available time spreads, and we note their separation is fairly uniform in this region. The ratio between the nearer in time spread to the more distant in time is normally about 1¼ when the first call to expire has 3 months to go. The ratio increases as the time to expiration shortens, but not rapidly, being about 1½ two months later. You may be able to spot a good spread by checking this ratio. If you are buying a long-time spread, depending on the decreasing time values to turn a profit, you should look for a ratio of at least 2 to 1 in order to pay the four commissions and have a chance of profit. Remember it is a low value of the longer-term spread you are looking to for the advantage, not an abnormally large value of the nearer-term spread. You look for a reduction in the opening debit and expect that this abnormality will disappear, together with the normal increase in spread value as time passes, to combine to produce a good profit at a lower risk than might otherwise be called for.

Figure 6–2 shows the spread values at the striking price of 45 for three values of volatility when the near call has 30 days until expiration and also at the time of its expiration. This chart illustrates the wide range of time spread values. It also shows the same general variation in time spread values for all volatilities. A better feel for the spread variations can be obtained by studying Table 6–3, which gives the results of opening two time spreads 30 days before the near call expires and closing when it does. Average commissions are applied. The results are

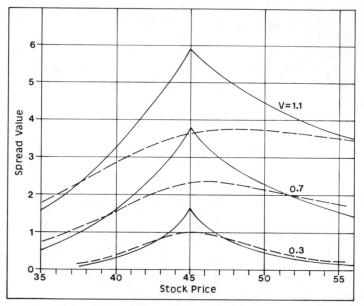

Figure 6–2.   Values of the balanced horizontal call spread as a function of stock price for different option volatilities V. The solid curve is the value at the time of expiration of the call sold, and the dashed curve for a time 30 days prior. The striking price is 45, and commissions are not included.

Table 6–3.   Time Spread Results

Time spreads opened when stock price was 40 by selling two calls 30 days from expiration and buying two expiring 3 months later, both at striking price of 45. Position is closed when first call expires. Gain or loss after average commissions is shown for prices of stock as indicated.

Stock Price When Position Closed	Option Volatility	Opening Cost	Received on Closing	Gain (%) or (Loss)
43	0.3	$ 87 − 15 = $ 72	$ 148	105
	0.7	313 − 33 = 280	503	80
	1.1	563 − 68 = 495	910	84
45	0.3	87 − 15 = 72	294	308
	0.7	313 − 33 = 280	713	155
	1.1	563 − 68 = 495	1132	129
47	0.3	87 − 15 = 72	121	68
	0.7	313 − 33 = 280	527	88
	1.1	563 − 68 = 495	971	96
50	0.3	87 − 15 = 72	5	(93)
	0.7	313 − 33 = 280	374	34
	1.1	563 − 68 = 495	805	63

56

given for various stock prices and low, medium, and high values of volatility. The maximum gain is obtained when the stock price equals the striking price on closing, but profits can be made if the stock price is within 2 or so points of the striking price.

The effect striking prices have on time spreads remains to be examined. If the stock price is expressed as a percentage of the striking price, the normal value of the calls is directly proportional to the striking price for a given volatility and time to expiration. It does not matter whether we choose low- or high-priced stocks in so far as percentage gains are concerned, except for the small variations introduced by the commission schedule.

As a practical example, if a stock was selling at 40, calls were available at a striking price of 45, and the calls for this stock had a $V = 0.7$, you could expect to be able to open a time spread for a debit of $1^9/_{16}$ points at a time when the near-term option had 30 days to expiration. If the stock increased 5 points in the next 30 days so as to yield the optimum gain, the spread value would be about $3^3/_4$ points. This optimum profit would amount to $2^3/_{16}$ points credit.

An alternative would be merely to purchase calls and hold for their appreciation in price. If the 120-day call had merely been purchased, it would have cost $2^1/_{16}$ points and would have been worth $3^3/_4$ points in 30 days at a stock price of 45, the same as the spread, for an overall gain of $1^{11}/_{16}$ points credit.

There are further considerations in evaluating your profit potential. Taking all factors into account, we would have a workout for the two situations as shown in Table 6–4. Typical commissions are assumed, and the workout is for two spread contracts, which reduces the commission cost per spread, and is the smallest number that should be considered. Commission costs will be further reduced if more contracts are opened at the same time. We see that the spread yields a greater profit than the outright purchase for this ideal situation. If the stock price is less than 45, the spread is better because of the sale of the short-term calls. If the stock price is greater than 45, your gain decreases for the spread, and the outright purchase continues to increase in value. In this example the spread decreases to the break-even point at a stock price of about 50 (see Figure 6–1, upper curve).

So far our discussions have been limited to the one-to-one spread with a 3-month time separation. There are other variations; for example, you could set up a spread with 6 months separation. Since the time value of options increases as the time to expiration increases, it would cost more to open the spread position and thus increase your risk. However, when you closed out the near-term short position, you could

Table 6–4. Workout for a Time Spread of Two Call Contracts
Compared with Outright Purchase of Two Calls—Commissions
Are Included

	Purchase Spread	Purchase Calls
At stock price of 40	Opening	
Buy two 45 calls at 2¹/₁₆ (120 days)	$445	$445
Sell two 45 calls at ¹/₂ (30 days)	90	
Net debit (risk)	355	445
At stock price of 45	Closing	
Sell two 45 calls at 3³/₄ (90 days)	713	713
Net gain	358	268
Profit (%)	100	60

hold the long positon and sell the next-to-expire option, setting up a new spread with 3 months separation, and eliminate part of the commission costs, provided the price relations and stock price movement are favorable for the new spread. Prediction of prices farther into the future is more difficult, and your risk of being wrong greater. In general, you are advised to deal only in 3-month time separations.

Your maximum risk in a horizontal spread is the opening cost, including commissions. In practice, it is somewhat less, for the option with the longer expiration time always has some value, except for a most extreme situation, at the time of expiration of the short option. Your maximum gain occurs when the stock price is at the striking price when the near-term option expires, but this exact situation cannot be expected to occur. The gain is dependent on the value of the long-term option at closing time, which varies from stock to stock, depending on price and volatility, and must be determined by finding its normal value. As a minimum, you should buy only spreads in which you could double your money after commissions if everything goes right. To the extent that price and timing predictions are questionable, you should increase your margin of safety. If you average 50% profit, you will be doing well.

VERTICAL CALL SPREADS

A vertical spread is initiated by buying an option at one striking price and selling another option at a different striking price, each having the same expiration date. There are several varieties of vertical spreads. If you are bullish, expecting the calls to increase in value, you would buy the lower striking price and sell the higher striking price. If the calls are held until expiration, your maximum gain would occur if the stock price is at or just below the higher striking price so that the call you sold will expire worthless but the one you purchased will have a value equal to the difference between the striking price and the stock price and can be sold. Your maximum profit would equal the striking price difference minus the cost of opening the spread, less commissions.

If you expect the stock to decrease in price, a bearish spread may be opened by selling calls with the lower striking price and buying the same number at the higher striking price. In this case, you will have a credit on the opening transaction. The margin requirement will amount to at least the spread difference, but your credit balance will partly offset this. In this case, you hope the stock will be below the lower striking price at expiration, and the opening credit will be your profit.

The one-to-one bullish or bearish spread assumes you have a feeling for the direction of price movement and that there is a good probability that the spread will work out advantageously. The spread position is a hedge that reduces your possible loss but at the same time also limits your maximum gain. Another form of vertical spread is the variable ratio, which can further limit losses. A popular form is one in which you sell two calls at one striking price for each one you buy at a lower striking price (a 2 to 1 ratio). Frequently, the prices are such that the credit from the sale of the two balances out the cost of the one. Sometimes one can even net a small credit after commissions. This has the very interesting feature that no matter how low the stock price may fall, you cannot lose. Of course you have to maintain the proper margin until the position is closed out. If the prices go up, as you should have expected if entering into this spread position, your maximum gain would occur if the option sold expires worthless and the price of the stock was at or slightly below the upper striking price. The long position could then be sold for maximum profit. The point of the stock price's being slightly below the striking price is based on the likelihood you would be inclined to cover the short position if the stock was very close to the striking price, rather than take a chance on having the call exercised and encountering additional commissions. If, at expiration, the stock price is anywhere between the lower and the upper striking prices, the position may be closed at a profit before commissions.

It is obvious that, in opening spread positions, you want to reduce the costs and increase the probability of gain. Also, the shorter the time taken to realize the expected gain, the greater the profits on an annualized basis. We now examine in some detail how option prices move, how to look for good spread positions, and when to close positions for a profit or to cut losses.

BALANCED BULLISH VERTICAL SPREAD

Consider first the simple one-to-one bullish spread. You sell one call at the higher striking price for each call purchased at the lower striking price. As usual, commissions are usually reduced per spread by dealing in multiple contracts. Refer to Figure 6–3, which plots the normal spread differential between calls of striking price 20 and 25 versus stock price as determined from the equations (2–2) and (2–3) for computing call values for a stock whose $V = 0.7$. Five values of time to expiration are shown: 0, 10, 30, 90, and 270 days. For low stock prices, the option with striking price of 25 has very little value. As the price increases toward 20, the lower striking price, the spread value increases as long as there is time remaining in the life of the options. If opening a call spread, the best values (smallest difference) are obtained when the stock price is low. Also, the spread is less for calls having a shorter time to expiration, but there may not be enough time for the price to rise sufficiently to realize a profit; watch this; check the price prediction.

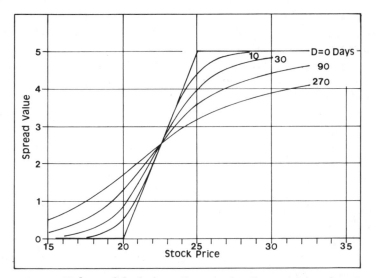

Figure 6–3.   Values of the balanced vertical call spread as a function of stock price for various times to expiration D at striking prices of 20 and 25. The option volatility is 0.7. Commissions are not included.

Table 6–5. Closing Spread Values

Vertical 1 : 1 closing spread values for calls when the stock price closed midway between the two striking prices, illustrating that the spread value is approximately half of the striking price difference and is independent of all other factors.

Date	Stock	Stock Price	Striking Prices	Spreads		
				July	Oct	Jan
5-11-77	Dig Eq	40	35–45	$4^7/_8$	$5^5/_{16}$	$5^7/_{16}$
5-12-77	Gt Wst	$22^1/_2$	20–25	$2^9/_{16}$	$2^3/_4$	$2^{13}/_{16}$
	Gulf O	$27^1/_2$	25–30	$1^{11}/_{16}$	$2^{13}/_{16}$	$2^1/_2$
5-13-77	John J	65	60–70	$5^1/_4$	$4^{11}/_{16}$	5
	Gulf O	$27^1/_2$	25–30	$2^5/_8$	$2^7/_8$	$2^5/_8$
	Merril	$17^1/_2$	15–20	$2^1/_4$	$2^1/_4$	$2^3/_8$
5-16-77	Hou OM	55	50–60	$4^5/_{16}$	$4^3/_8$	$4^1/_2$
	Gulf O	$27^1/_2$	25–30	$2^3/_4$	$2^{11}/_{16}$	$2^{11}/_{16}$

Note that the spread value is 2.5 for a stock price of 22.5. In general, all 1 : 1 vertical spreads have a normal value of half of the difference between the striking prices when the stock is midway between these striking prices (see Table 6–5, which illustrates this point by giving the spread values in terms of the closing call prices, in the July-Oct-Jan series, for those cases in which the stock closing price was exactly midway between two striking prices, having quoted call prices for the three time periods). This price relation exists regardless of time to expiration, option volatility, or level of striking prices. It is therefore a useful and dependable bench mark in evaluating vertical spread values.

As the stock price increases, the spread value increases to a maximum of the difference between the striking prices, which is reached only when the price is very high or the time is very near expiration and the price at or above the upper striking price. It usually is to your advantage to close out a spread when expiration approaches if the stock is near the upper striking price and put your money to work elsewhere. Also you avoid a possible reversal in price that could cut your profits, and if the price continues upward, you want to avoid exercise, which would cost greater commissions. You may find prices such that the higher striking price call, which you are selling, is overvalued or the one you are buying is undervalued, thus giving rise to a more favorable spread.

Figure 6–4 shows the effect of volatility. The opening spread differential is less for low volatilities than for higher volatilities, and the

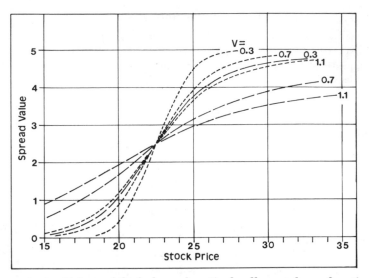

Figure 6–4.   Values of the balanced vertical call spread as a function of stock price for various values of option volatilities V for times to expiration of 30 (dotted curve) and 270 (dashed curve) days. Striking prices are 20 and 25. Commissions are not included.

closing spread values increase faster above the upper striking price. These relationships favor the lower option volatilities. In general, the underlying stock volatility for these options is also lower, and the stock is less likely to make large moves. You must appraise the chances for the stock price to move the required amount in the time desired. The figures represent only normal valued options. In practice, there are variations from these values that may work for or against you.

It is interesting to note from Figure 6–3 and 6–4 that the spread values range between 3 and 4 at the upper striking price, if not too close to expiration, for the 5-point separation of striking prices. For 10-point separation, it would be 6 to 8, etc. This gives you a good range of values to watch for if wanting to close the spread position. It is often better to take a moderate profit and put your money to work elsewhere, making more turnovers per year.

If you open a spread for 1½ and closed for 3, you would have about a 75% gain after commissions when using 5-point striking price differences. By being choosy, you may do better than this on opening, and if the price increases somewhat above midway between the striking prices, you can get 3 or better without having to wait for expiration and the maximum gain. The conditions are much less critical than for the horizontal spread. You must find a stock that promises a good price increase, but it can be at any rate as long as it occurs before expiration. It cannot move too fast, nor do you have to worry about an overshoot, though profits should be taken when available rather than waiting for expiration, for your money can be put to greater advantage elsewhere. The best opening positions occur when the stock price is a little below the lower striking price and the time to expiration is not too great, but do not push your luck too far; leave enough time for your stock to advance the expected amount.

You do not open a bullish vertical spread, instead of merely buying the call, just to use a fancy strategy. You choose the spread because it costs less, thus reducing your risk. When the stock price is low compared with the striking price, the calls you would sell short may not be worth much; their only value is to cut your cash outlay. If this is not appreciable, forget them, for they can cause you problems if the price goes up to or beyond the upper striking price. Your commissions increase if you have to cover them, they limit your maximum profit, and they could be exercised.

Table 6–6 gives spread values for the CBOE January and April calls as of November 20, 1976, when the stock price is near the lower striking price. As Figure 6–3 indicates, the lower values are found in the first options to expire (January). The quoted closing call prices for the call sold are rather small when the spread is small. You must evaluate whether this sort of spread is worthwhile or should you merely purchase a call. There is no evaluation of whether any of the spreads listed in Table 6–6 are desirable from a price-time movement. You could find that the near-term spread, having the lowest value, would not have time to achieve your price objective. If you have to use a spread having a longer time to expiration, the call sold generally has a significant value that may make the spread more attractive than merely purchasing a call.

Table 6–7 gives vertical spread values of the CBOE January series as of January 14, 1977, one week before expiration, for those stocks listed in Table 6–6. None of these spreads reached the maximum value, over half would have lost money, and none would have been very profitable after commissions. This illustrates how important it is to find a stock that will increase in price an appreciable amount before the option expires. Of the group of April expirations, only two would have proved fully successful. As of April 14, the day before expiration, Homestake Mining reached 40⅝, requiring covering of the short call, and RCA reached 29⅝, the short call expiring worthless. Each netted 3⅛ points profit before commissions.

At times you have a choice as to whether to use a 5- or 10-point

Table 6–6. Call and Vertical Spread Values, as of November 20, 1976, for the CBOE Stocks Priced near the Lower Striking Price

Stock	Stock Price	Call	Call Price	Call	Call Price	1:1 Spread
Bank Am	$25^1/8$	Jan 25	1	Jan 30	$^1/_{16}$	$^{15}/_{16}$
		Apr 25	$1^1/_2$	Apr 30	$^5/_{16}$	$1^3/_{16}$
Bruns	$14^1/_2$	Jan 15	$^5/_8$	Jan 20	$^1/_8$	$^1/_2$
		Apr 15	$1^3/_{16}$	Apr 20	$^3/_8$	$^{13}/_{16}$
Burl N	44	Jan 45	$1^9/_{16}$	Jan 50	$^1/_4$	$1^5/_{16}$
		Apr 45	$2^{15}/_{16}$	Apr 50	$1^1/_4$	$1^{11}/_{16}$
Citicp	$29^5/_8$	Jan 30	$1^1/_{16}$	Jan 35	$^3/_{16}$	$^7/_8$
		Apr 30	2	Apr 35	$^9/_{16}$	$1^7/_{16}$
Delta	$35^5/_8$	Jan 35	$2^3/_8$	Jan 40	$^7/_{16}$	$1^{15}/_{16}$
		Apr 35	$3^5/_8$	Apr 40	$1^1/_4$	$2^3/_8$
Dow Ch	$39^5/_8$	Jan 40	$1^7/_8$	Jan 45	$^7/_{16}$	$1^7/_{16}$
		Apr 40	$3^1/_8$	Apr 45	$1^5/_{16}$	$1^{13}/_{16}$
Exxon	$50^1/_4$	Jan 50	$1^{15}/_{16}$	Jan 55	$^3/_8$	$1^9/_{16}$
		Apr 50	3	Apr 55	$1^1/_{16}$	$1^{15}/_{16}$
Fluor	36	Jan 35	$2^5/_{16}$	Jan 40	$^5/_8$	$1^{11}/_{16}$
		Apr 35	$3^3/_4$	Apr 40	$1^1/_2$	$2^1/_4$
G M	$70^5/_8$	Jan 70	$2^7/_8$	Jan 80	$^1/_4$	$2^5/_8$
		Apr 70	$4^1/_4$	Apr 80	$^7/_8$	$3^3/_8$
Homstk	$35^3/_4$	Jan 35	$2^3/_4$	Jan 40	$^{13}/_{16}$	$1^{15}/_{16}$
		Apr 35	$3^3/_4$	Apr 40	$1^7/_8$	$1^7/_8$
ITT	$30^3/_4$	Jan 30	$1^9/_{16}$	Jan 35	$^1/_4$	$1^5/_{16}$
		Apr 30	$2^7/_{16}$	Apr 35	$^9/_{16}$	$1^7/_8$
John J	80	Jan 80	$2^1/_2$	Jan 90	$^1/_2$	2
		Apr 80	5	Apr 90	$1^1/_2$	$3^1/_2$
Kerr M	69	Jan 70	$2^1/_2$	Jan 80	$^1/_4$	$2^1/_4$
		Apr 70	$4^1/_2$	Apr 80	$^3/_4$	$3^3/_4$
Nw Air	$29^1/_2$	Jan 30	$1^1/_8$	Jan 35	$^1/_4$	$^7/_8$
		Apr 30	2	Apr 35	$^3/_4$	$1^1/_4$
Pennz	$31^3/_4$	Jan 30	$1^7/_8$	Jan 35	$^3/_8$	$1^1/_2$
		Apr 30	$2^5/_8$	Apr 35	$^{15}/_{16}$	$1^{11}/_{16}$
Pepsi	79	Jan 80	$2^1/_2$	Jan 90	$^3/_{16}$	$2^5/_{16}$
		Apr 80	$3^3/_4$	Apr 90	$1^1/_4$	$2^1/_2$
RCA	$25^1/8$	Jan 25	$1^3/_8$	Jan 30	$^3/_{16}$	$1^3/_{16}$
		Apr 25	$2^1/_{16}$	Apr 30	$^{11}/_{16}$	$1^3/_8$
Sperry	$44^1/8$	Jan 45	$1^7/_8$	Jan 50	$^1/_4$	$1^5/_8$
		Apr 45	$2^{15}/_{16}$	Apr 50	$1^1/_8$	$1^{13}/_{16}$
Tex In	$98^7/_8$	Jan 100	$5^1/_4$	Jan 110	$1^3/_4$	$3^1/_2$
		Apr 100	$8^5/_8$	Apr 110	4	$4^5/_8$

spread, or occasionally greater, in a given stock. This may allow you to make a better match to the price-time projection of the stock. You may also be able to save some on commissions for a given profit when using the larger spread.

Table 6-7. Values of January Calls and Vertical Spreads as
of January 14, 1977, One Week before Expiration, for Those
Stocks Listed in Table 6-6

Stock	Stock Price	Call	Call Price	Call	Call Price	1:1 Spread
Bank Am	28 1/8	Jan 25	2 7/8	Jan 30	1/16	2 13/16
Bruns	15 5/8	Jan 15	11/16	Jan 20	1/16	5/8
Bur N	43 3/4	Jan 45	2 1/8	Jan 50	. . .	2 1/8
Citicp	32 3/4	Jan 30	2 7/8	Jan 35	1/16	2 13/16
Delta	37 1/4	Jan 35	2 1/8	Jan 40	1/16	2 1/16
Dow Ch	40 5/8	Jan 40	3/4	Jan 45	1/16	11/16
Exxon	52 1/2	Jan 50	2 9/16	Jan 55	1/16	2 1/2
Fluor	36	Jan 35	1 1/4	Jan 40	1/16	1 3/16
G M	75 1/4	Jan 70	5 1/4	Jan 80	1/16	5 3/16
Homstk	35 5/8	Jan 35	13/16	Jan 40	1/16	3/4
ITT	33 3/4	Jan 30	3 3/4	Jan 35	1/16	3 11/16
John J	73 3/4	Jan 80	1/16	Jan 90	. . .	1/16
Kerr M	70 3/8	Jan 70	1 1/4	Jan 80	1/16	1 3/16
Nw Air	28 1/8	Jan 30	1/8	Jan 35	. . .	1/8
Pennz	33 3/8	Jan 30	3 1/8	Jan 35	1/8	3
Pepsi	77 7/8	Jan 80	1/4	Jan 90	. . .	1/4
RCA	26 1/8	Jan 25	1 3/16	Jan 30	1/16	1 1/8
Sperry	40 1/2	Jan 45	1/16	Jan 50	1/16	0
Tex In	94 3/8	Jan 100	3/16	Jan 110	1/16	1/8

The balanced bullish vertical spread is preferred over the horizontal spread for most situations. For optimum profits, both require purchase at a stock price that is expected to appreciate with time. The vertical spread does not care how fast the price rises, nor how slowly, as long as the objective is reached before the options expire, though a fast rise allows profits to be taken, and your funds can be turned over more times a year. The horizontal spread, in contrast, requires the stock price to rise such that it is near the striking price at expiration time, a very critical requirement. If the price rises too fast, you have to close your position for less than optimum gain, or even at a loss, but in the vertical spread there is no danger from a stock price overshoot. The opening and closing spread values are easily determined for the vertical spread, but they are dependent on price and option volatility for horizontal spreads, making analysis more complicated.

If the price is not expected to move, the vertical spread cannot produce a gain, but, in theory, a horizontal spread can by taking a position in the far out calls near the striking price and holding for the decrease in time to expiration to increase the spread value. The problem is being sure the stock price will be near the striking price after some fairly long period of time.

BALANCED BEARISH VERTICAL SPREAD

If you expect the price of a stock to decrease, you can enter into a bearish call spread by selling an option at one striking price and buying another at a higher striking price that expires at the same time. In this case you have a net credit balance, but you will have to supply margin equal to the difference in striking prices, a part of which is offset by the credit on the transaction. Your normal expectation is that both calls will expire worthless and you can pocket the initial credit.

If the stock should increase in price, you will be faced with closing your position at a cost of the difference between the striking prices plus commissions. These costs, less your credit on opening the spread, represent your maximum risk. Obviously the greater the credit you can achieve on opening the spread, the less the risk, and the greater the possible gain. You can determine this risk reward ratio before placing your opening order, and it becomes a factor in selecting bearish spread candidates along with the prediction of stock price movement.

The bearish spread, unlike the bullish spread, is entered into in order to put an upper limit on your risk, which you would not have if only selling a call. Your credit is decreased to pay for limiting the risk. This function contrasts with the bullish spread, which merely reduces cost.

We may use the curves in Figures 6–3 and 6–4 in a reverse sense to their use for the bullish spread. We must plan to open the spread when the options have enough time to expiration for the stock to fall sufficiently to reduce the spread value to where a profit can be made even if the short call has to be covered. An average selection would be to establish a little over 3 points credit for striking price separations of 5 points at a stock price slightly below the upper striking price. Disregarding commissions, your risk reward ratio would then be about 2 to 3, and after commissions no better than about even. You should search for better situations than this, but do not be trapped into a large credit on opening that is due to short time to expiration unless the stock price analysis clearly indicates the stock has time to achieve the lower price objective needed to be able to retain this credit.

If the price falls rapidly enough, you may want to close out the spread by selling your long call and covering (buying) your short call. Considerations are how much additional profit you can achieve if holding until expiration weighed against closing the position to free margin for use elsewhere to greater advantage. Also, the projected stock price movement may become unfavorable for holding. If it appears that the price may reverse and move upward, it could be advantageous to close the position. As in the bullish spread, you sometimes have a choice of a greater spread between striking prices than the 5 points.

Like the bullish spread discussed in the previous section, the price-time movement is not critical, as with horizontal spreads. You need only to find a stock that is expected to decrease sufficiently in price by expiration time. The faster it moves downward, the better, for you can realize most of your maximum profit potential by closing your position and put your money to work elsewhere. There is no danger from a downward overshoot in stock price, though you will realize less than optimum profit.

VARIABLE RATIO VERTICAL SPREAD

In opening a spread position, you do not need to sell the same number of option contracts as you purchase but may establish any ratio you consider appropriate. A common spread is the sale of two options at the upper striking price for each one purchased at a lower striking price in a vertical spread. This ratio spread can be executed for a relatively small cash outlay, including commissions, or even for a credit, depending on the circumstances. You will, however, have to meet the margin requirements. In this case, one short option is margined against the long position, and the other is a naked sale. You open this spread expecting the stock price to be near the upper striking price at expiration, at which the spread has its maximum value. The long call would then be worth about the spread difference and can be sold, but the short (higher striking price) calls expire worthless. Your downside risk is small and limited to the initial cash outlay. Disregarding commissions, the stock price can move upward to a level above the upper striking price, equal to the difference between the striking prices, before you sustain a loss at expiration. If the stock price is anywhere between this upper level and the lower striking price, you would have a credit on closing. Considering typical commissions and the opening cost, the workout for a bullish spread at various stock prices at expiration time is as illustrated in Table 6–8. As of March 29, 1976, Homestake Mining closed at 38¾, its July 40 call sold at 3, and its July 45 call at 1½. Assume you purchased two July 40 calls and sold four July 45s. Typical commissions are about $83, which is your cash outlay and downside risk. Your maximum

Table 6–8. Workout for the 2 : 1 Vertical Bullish Spread for Homestake Mining Assuming the Purchase of Two July 40 Calls and Sale of Four July 45 Calls for a Zero Debit before Commissions

Stock Price	Value of Two July 40s	Value of Four July 45s	Net before Commissions	Total Commissions	Net after Commissions
40	$ 0	$ 0	$ 0	$ 83	$ −83
41	200	0	200	112	88
42	400	0	400	115	285
43	600	0	600	118	482
44	800	0	800	121	679
45	1000	0	1000	124	876
46	1200	400	800	172	628
47	1400	800	600	180	420
48	1600	1200	400	189	211
49	1800	1600	200	197	3
50	2000	2000	0	206	−206

possible profit is $876, and you make a profit if the stock price, at expiration of the July calls, is between about 41 and 49. If the stock moves higher in price, you begin to lose greater amounts at expiration. You should close out your position early if the price moves up too rapidly. Figure 6–5 shows normal values for a 2-to-1 spread before commissions for a stock having an option volatility of 0.7 for various times to expiration. This figure illustrates how accurate your price-time prediction must be in order to achieve near maximum profits. If, for the assumptions used here, the price is off by 1 point, the spread value drops from 5 to 4 at expiration. If the price moves up too rapidly and you feel the need to close out your position, the spread has rather limited value until it is near the expiration time. Further, the best place to close out the spread is below the upper striking price, and the longer the time to expiration, the further below is this optimum price.

Three strategies are suggested by these curves. A bullish spread, as described above and illustrated in Table 6–8, is opened below the lower striking price when you expect a strong upward move in the stock price to near the upper striking price in about the time the calls have to go to expiration.

A second, which is neutral, is to open the spread at a point near the upper striking price with the expectation that the price will remain nearly constant until the options expire. As an example, using Figure 6–5, at a time around 2 to 3 months before expiration, you should have

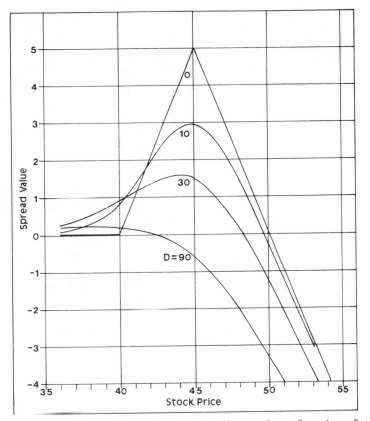

Figure 6–5. Values of the 2 : 1 vertical call spread as a function of stock price for different times to expiration *D* and striking prices of 40 and 45. Option volatility is 0.7, and commissions are not included.

little, if any, cash outlay; so the downside risk can be very limited, or perhaps even a small credit can be established. The value of the calls sold short will be essentially due to the time value, which will disappear as expiration is approached. The calls purchased will have an intrinsic value up to the difference in striking prices if the stock price at expiration is at the upper striking price, thus resulting in maximum profits.

A third strategy is bearish, and the spread would be opened when the stock price is above the upper striking price for a net credit, with the expectation that the stock price will fall, either allowing you to close the position for a cost less than the opening credit or, in the extreme, for all options to expire worthless (stock below the lower striking price), resulting in your initial credit becoming the profit on the transaction. The optimum circumstance is for the price to be at the upper striking price so that the calls sold short expire worthless, but the long calls have value that can add to profits by their sale. In this strategy there is no downside risk. The upside risk is the value of one short call at the final stock price, which is not limited, plus the difference in striking prices—the other short call is offset by the one long call—less the opening credit.

The variable ratio spread permits opening for a very low, if any, cost that is likewise your downside risk. It also provides an extended price range over which there is upside protection, beyond which the risk is unlimited. You can, however, control your loss in this respect by closing the position early at a moderate loss. You pay for these advantages in having to be more precise in price timing if you are to achieve a good profit; the stock price must be near the upper striking price at expiration if following a bullish or neutral strategy. In all strategies, margin is required.

The bearish strategy is less critical, only requiring the stock price to fall far enough to avoid closing costs, though you will not have much gain unless the stock price is near the upper striking price. This strategy should be discarded in favor of the balanced one-to-one spread previously discussed, in which you open with a credit that can be retained if the stock price simply falls far enough. Also, the upside risk is limited to the striking price difference in the balanced bearish spread but becomes unlimited after the protected area of the ratio spread is passed.

RATIO HORIZONTAL CALL SPREAD

Another spread variation is the *variable ratio horizontal spread*, in which the long and short positions are not in balance. You might sell twice as many of the first to expire options as you buy of the longer-term options. This may result in opening the positions with no debit or even a credit, with risk against a decrease in stock price being completely eliminated. Of course, you have to meet the margin requirements. Half of the short calls are sold naked and therefore require full margin. The other half are margined against the long position.

In the balanced spread, discussed previously, your risk was limited to the initial cash outlay to establish the spread position. If the stock moved down, the worst that could happen is for both calls to expire worthless. If the stock moved upward, the long call, having more time to expiration, would be worth more than the short call; so you could not lose any more, and your risk is fixed. With the ratio spread it is different when the stock moves up. With only a limited movement above the striking price the cost of covering the greater number of short calls exceeds what you could obtain for the long calls; the risk is not limited.

If the stock price stays below the striking price, the ratio spread produces greater profits, since the opening position costs less, but this is realized at the expense of involving unlimited risk. You can increase the ratio to, say, 3 to 1 and have a chance of even greater profits but at a greater risk. In fact, any ratio may be chosen, depending on your analysis of the expected price movement. Ratios of 3 to 2, 4 to 3, etc., are not uncommon.

The ratio horizontal spread variation has little to offer. It is just as difficult to estimate the expected gain as in the balanced spread. The gain is determined by the value of the long call when the short-term call expires, and this value is dependent on the stock price and volatility. Though the cost may be eliminated, you have a naked call to margin; so capital is tied up.

DIAGONAL SPREADS

A vertical spread can be combined with a horizontal spread to form a *diagonal spread*; that is, you purchase a call at one striking price and sell another at a different striking price expiring at a different time. There are four different combinations. Assume calls are available at striking prices of 40 and 45 for both the April and July expirations; then the combinations are

1. Sell Apr 40 and buy July 45
2. Sell Apr 45 and buy July 40
3. Buy Apr 40 and sell July 45
4. Buy Apr 45 and sell July 40

In the first two combinations, the short call can be margined against the long calls. Further variations can be established by using either 3- or 6-month time separations and introducing variable ratios. These types of spreads are more complex to analyze and monitor and do not offer advantages over what can be accomplished with simpler spreads.

PUT SPREADS

For all the call spreads we have discussed, there is a corresponding put spread. They have similar properties and therefore double the pos-

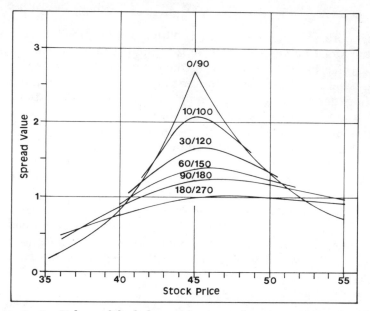

Figure 6–6. Values of the balanced horizontal put spread as a function of stock price for various times to expiration of the short put when the long put has 90 additional days to go. The striking price is 45, and option volatility is 0.6.

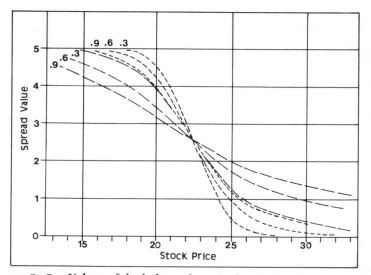

Figure 6–7. Values of the balanced vertical put spread as a function of stock price for various values of option volatilities for times to expiration of 30 (dotted curve) and 270 (dashed curve) days. Striking prices are 20 and 25.

72

sibilities available. You should examine the alternatives for the most favorable price combination. Available striking prices may favor one or the other as well as variations in option prices.

In general, if bullish, you would select call spreads, and if bearish, put spreads. As an illustration, refer to Figure 6–1. If bullish, you would open a horizontal call spread near the stock price of 40 for about 1½ points when there are 30 days to go. If bearish, you could open a call spread near the stock price of 50 for about 2 points, somewhat more costly. However, you have an alternative in puts (see Figure 6–6 for corresponding put spread values). Since horizontal spread values vary with the option volatility and the put and call volatilities are frequently somewhat different, this becomes a consideration in selecting the type of spread.

Figure 6–7 illustrates the way the balanced vertical put spread varies, corresponding to Figure 6–4. We discussed previously how one can use the vertical call spread for either a bullish or bearish position, opening for a debit if bullish and a credit if bearish. The vertical put spread reverses the situation; that is, when bullish you sell at the higher striking price for an opening credit, expecting the stock price to increase to where both puts are worthless at expiration or reach a low value where it would be advantageous to close the position. If bearish, the lower striking price is sold and the higher-cost upper striking price put purchased for a net debit.

Margin is required for bearish call and bullish put spreads; that is, if opening for a credit, margin is required, but if opening the position creates a debit, no margin is required. The capital required may be somewhat different for the two alternatives. Alternative positions are illustrated using Santa Fe International, which closed at a price of 50⅞ on June 6, 1977, having given a buy signal, closing the bullish position and opening a bearish position on June 29 at a price of 55, and finally closing out on July 28 at 50¼.

Bullish Call Spread

Open spread June 6, 1977;
  stock price 50⅞

Buy 2 Oct 50 calls at 4⅞		$ 975 debit
Sell 2 Oct 55 calls at 2⅜		475 credit
Commissions		74 debit
Net cost	$ 574	

Close spread June 29, 1977;
  stock price 55

Sell 2 Oct 50 calls at 7		$1400 credit
Buy 2 Oct 55 calls at 3⅝		725 debit
Commissions		83 debit
Net credit	$ 592	
Gain	18 (3%)	

Bullish Put Spread

Open spread June 6, 1977;
  stock price 50⅞

Buy 2 Oct 50 puts at 3⅜		$ 675 debit
Sell 2 Oct 55 puts at 6¼		1250 credit
Commissions		81 debit
Net credit	$ 494	
Margin	1000	

Close spread June 29, 1977;
  stock price 55

Sell 2 Oct 50 puts at 1		$ 200 credit
Buy 2 Oct 55 puts at 2⅞		575 debit
Commissions		64 debit
Net debit	$ 439	
Gain	55	

Bearish Call Spread

Open spread June 29, 1977;
  stock price 55

Sell 2 Oct 50 calls at 7		$1400 credit
Buy 2 Oct 55 calls at 3⅝		725 debit
Commissions		83 debit
Net credit	$ 592	
Margin	1000	

Close spread July 28, 1977;
  stock price 50¼

Buy 2 Oct 50 calls at 3⅜		$ 675 debit
Sell 2 Oct 55 calls at 1½		300 credit
Commissions		67 debit
Net debit	$ 442	
Gain	150	

Bearish Put Spread

Open spread June 29, 1977;
 stock price 55

Buy 2 Oct 55 puts at 2⅞		$ 575 debit
Sell 2 Oct 50 puts at 1		200 credit
Commissions		64 debit
Net cost	$ 439	

Close spread July 28, 1977;
 stock price 50¼

Sell 2 Oct 55 puts at 5⅜		$1075 credit
Buy 2 Oct 50 puts at 2¼		450 debit
Commissions		74 debit
Net credit	$ 551	
Gain	112 (25%)	

The 2 to 1 ratio vertical spread using calls, that is, selling two calls at one striking price for each purchased at a lower striking price, had the characteristics of low cost, the downside risk limited to the cost, if any, and no upside risk until the stock price exceeds a value above the upper striking price by an amount equal to the difference between the two striking prices. A corresponding put spread can be opened by selling two puts at one striking price for each purchased at a higher striking price. Maximum gain occurs in each case if the options expire when the stock price is at the striking price of the two options sold. For the put spread, it is the upside risk that is determined by the opening cost, and protection is obtained on the downside to a stock price below the lower striking price by an amount of the difference between striking prices. Your selection of call or put spread might be based on which price direction you want to have no risk, other than the opening cost, if any.

BUTTERFLY SPREAD

The *butterfly* or *sandwich* spread is a combination of particular interest when it can be established advantageously. Three striking prices at the same expiration date are required. You sell two calls at the middle striking price for each one you buy at the lower and upper prices. This has the interesting feature of showing a profit on expiration if the stock price is anywhere between the lower and upper striking prices and being of zero value for any price outside of this range, neglecting commission costs. On occasion, the option prices have been so related that the spread could have been opened with a small credit, in fact enough to cover commissions, both opening and closing, in which case you could hardly lose. You have to worry only about a possible early exercise of the short calls. The margin required is low. One short call is fully margined against the long call at the lower striking price, requiring only the minimum spread margin, if any, and the other short call is margined against the call at the upper striking price, requiring only the spread difference as margin. Stocks normally having wide daily swings in price are candidates for establishing butterfly spreads, one leg at a time, with a small overall credit balance; so you cannot lose except possibly for added commissions if there is an early exercise.

The butterfly spread works because at expiration the long call at the lower striking price has enough intrinsic value just to balance the two short call's intrinsic values at the upper striking price, and for higher prices the intrinsic values of the long and short calls move together with a zero balance. This is illustrated in Table 6–9 for a butterfly spread with striking prices of 40, 45, and 50. At expiration, neglecting commissions, the results are as shown.

A variation occurs when striking prices are not available with the same separation. For example, for striking prices of 45, 50, and 60, you

Table 6–9. Value of a Butterfly Call Spread as a Function of Price at Expiration

Stock Price	One Long Call $S = 40$	Two Short Calls $S = 45$	One Long Call $S = 50$	Net
40 (or less)	0	0	0	0
41	100	0	0	100
42	200	0	0	200
43	300	0	0	300
44	400	0	0	400
45	500	0	0	500
46	600	−200	0	400
47	700	−400	0	300
48	800	−600	0	200
49	900	−800	0	100
50	1000	−1000	0	0
51	1100	−1200	100	0
52	1200	−1400	200	0

can set up a spread having the same desirable characteristics. In this case buy two 45s, sell three 50s, and buy one 60. Your profit range is for stock prices between 45 and 60 with the maximum at 50. This, in fact, offers some advantages. It increases the range of stock prices by 5 points over which you have a gain before commissions and offers with six calls the same maximum gain as with two standard butterflies requiring eight calls. The disadvantage is that it would require a little more cash to open (see Figure 6–9 and compare with Figure 6–8); also there are fewer classes of options with the required number of striking prices.

You may use the butterfly in either a bullish or bearish situation. If bullish on the stock, the opening spread would be made at a price near or below the lower striking price. For normal prices this would require a net debit, as may be seen from the curves in Figure 6–8. As the price moves up, the spread value increases, reaching a maximum of 5 points (for 5-point spread differences) at expiration if the stock price is at the middle striking price. You may want to close your position early if the price appears to be moving too rapidly. This should be done near the center striking price.

If bearish, you would open the spread near the upper striking price. You expect the stock price to fall to near the center striking price by expiration time. The commission costs for this spread will be somewhat higher because the stock price is above the striking price of the short

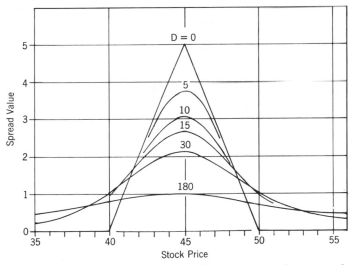

Figure 6–8.   Values of the butterfly call spread as a function of stock price for different values of time to expiration *D* before commissions. Option volatility is 0.7.

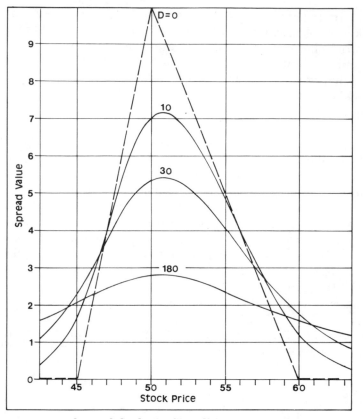

Figure 6–9. Values of the butterfly call spread as a function of stock price for different values of time to expiration *D* for an unequal separation of striking prices. These curves are for the purchase of two calls at a striking price of 45, sale of three at 50, and purchase of one at 60. Option volatility is 0.6. Commissions are not included.

calls. Remember the exercise call looks only at your short position. Holding a spread gives no added protection against an exercise.

The butterfly spread may be set up with puts instead of calls. You sell two puts at the middle striking price and purchase one at the lower and another at the upper striking prices. If bearish, you would open the position when the stock price was near the upper striking price in the hope it would fall to about the middle striking price or slightly above, so that the two puts sold short would expire worthless along with the long one at the low striking price. The put at the highest striking price could be sold for a profit. For this bearish position the option values are lower at the high stock price; so commissions will be somewhat less on

Table 6–10. Possible Put and Call Butterfly Spreads as of
July 28, 1977, Assuming Execution at the Quoted Closing
Prices—Commissions Are Not Taken into Account

Stock and Price	Striking Price	Option Price	Butter-fly	Option Price	Butter-fly	Option Price	Butter-fly
IBM	240	27		29³/₈		32	
267³/₈	260	11³/₈	7¹/₈	15³/₈	6¹/₈	18³/₈	4⁷/₈
	280	2⁷/₈		7¹/₂		9⁵/₈	
	240p	¹³/₁₆		2¹/₂		3⁷/₈	
	260p	4³/₄	6¹³/₁₆	7¹/₂	5³/₈	9⁵/₈	3³/₈
	280p	15¹/₂		17⁷/₈		18³/₄	
Mesa Pt	35	10³/₈		11			
44	40	6	1¹/₂	7¹/₂	⁵/₈		
	45	3¹/₈		4⁵/₈			
	35p	³/₈		¹¹/₁₆			
	40p	1¹/₁₆	1¹/₄	1³/₄	1¹³/₁₆		
	45p	3		4⁵/₈			
San Fe	45	6³/₄		7⁷/₈			
50¹/₄	50	3³/₈	1¹/₂	4³/₄	1¹/₈		
	55	1¹/₂		2³/₄			
	45p	¹³/₁₆		1³/₈			
	50p	2¹/₄	1¹¹/₁₆	3¹/₄	1¹/₄		
	55p	5³/₈		6³/₈			

opening, and this could be a small advantage over a bearish position in calls. Other things being equal, one would use calls for a bullish position and puts for a bearish position.

There are other considerations in whether calls or puts are choosen for a butterfly spread. One may have the three striking prices available and the other not. The deviations from normal values may favor puts or calls, allowing lower opening costs. Finally, if your stock price movement prediction indicates a price less than, or greater than, the middle striking price at expiration time, choose the combination that would avoid having to cover the short options at the middle striking price; that is, if bullish and you expect the stock price to overshoot the middle striking price, it might be better to use puts to avoid the commissions associated with covering two short calls.

Table 6–10 shows a number of possible butterfly spreads with opening cost before commissions for purpose of illustration, using quoted closing price. Whether it would have been desirable to open such spreads would be based on an analysis of the expected underlying stock movement. Puts are designated by a p following the striking price. Making a good profit in either a put or call butterfly is difficult. The position needs to be held to expiration, and the stock price needs to be very close to the middle striking price. Also, commissions are greater because of the large number of options involved.

7 Straddles and Related Combinations

—Combining puts and calls
—You can bet on both sides

We have discussed how, in general, calls are purchased when you are bullish and puts are purchased when you are bearish on a stock. You can thus take a position on either side of the market. You can also combine a put and a call to form what is known as a *straddle*. Straddles can be bought or sold as a unit by merely specifying the total price. They can, of course, be formed one part at a time, and either the call or put may be sold or covered individually, leaving you with a position in the other option. Straddles cost the same as the combined cost of the put and the call, and commissions are usually computed on each individually. The term *straddle* is applied only to the combination of the purchase or sale of equal numbers of puts and calls at the same striking price and expiration date.

WHEN TO BUY A STRADDLE

We have stressed the point that you should take an option position only after analyzing the underlying stock and determining that it has good near-term prospects to move in a predictable direction. A straddle does not give you a reason to know any less about the stock, but it does allow you to take advantage of the special situation in which a stock makes rapid and wide moves in both directions. If the price swings are great enough, you may purchase a straddle and expect the price to move enough so that a profit may be made by selling the call if the price moves up or by selling the put if the price moves down. You would be left with the other option, which you could sell at a loss to close out your position if this is desired, or you might want to hold it for the reverse swing, expecting to make a profit on it also.

We have seen that the shape of the option curves are such that there is a rapid change in slope near where the stock price goes through the striking price, particularly when the time to expiration is not too long. The slope changes in such a way that the value of the option, put or call, changes by a greater amount in the in-the-money region than in the out-of-the-money region. If we assume that a straddle is purchased at the striking price, then as the price moves away from this point, one option will move to in-the-money, and the other to out-of-the-money. The increase in value of the one moving to in-the-money will be greater than the loss on the one moving to out-of-the-money. The straddle value will therefore increase for a stock price move in either direction from the striking price. This is illustrated in Figure 7–1. When the increase in value is enough to overcome commissions, the straddle may be sold at a profit. Figure 7–1 shows values for different times to expiration, when both the put and call have an option volatility of 0.6.

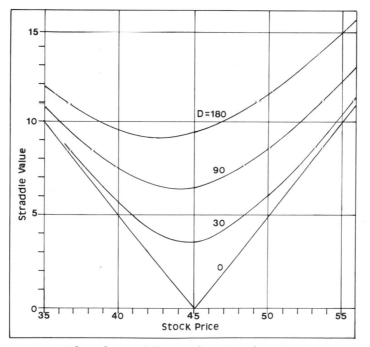

Figure 7–1. Value of a straddle as a function of stock price around the striking price of 45 for different times to expiration. The option volatility is 0.6.

The maximum risk on the purchase of a straddle is the opening cost plus commissions. To suffer this maximum risk, the options would have to expire with the stock price at the striking price. Although this is improbable, the straddle may not be worth much as expiration approaches. If the stock price is near the striking price, the time values will have largely disappeared, and you are left with only one option having an intrinsic value. When expiration is approaching, you should close your position on any significant price swing away from the striking price.

When a stock on which you have purchased a straddle makes wide daily swings, you may want to place an open sell order at the price you would accept. Rapid turnovers may be achieved in this manner, and good profits made on a yearly basis for modest individual gains.

Figure 7–2 shows the dependence of straddle value on option vol-

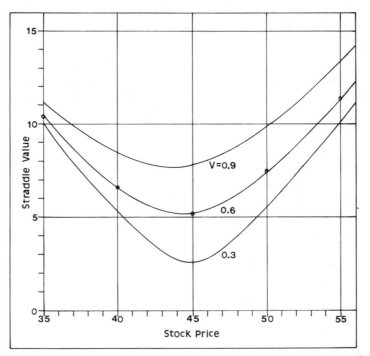

Figure 7–2.   Straddle value as a function of stock price at a striking price of 45 for different option volatilities. The option volatility is the same for both put and call, except the plotted circles are for volatilities of 0.5 for the put and 0.7 for the call, resulting in a straddle value corresponding to the average of 0.6. Time to expiration is 60 days.

atility, the minimum value being much less for a low volatility than for a high volatility. At the striking price, the straddle value is all time value, but as the stock price moves away from the striking price, the increase in value is largely due to one option gaining in intrinsic value so that the overall straddle value is not so dependent on volatility. It would be good strategy to select low-volatility straddles for purchase if the stock can be expected to move a sufficient number of points from the striking price in time to take profits before the options expire. It is also desirable that the price movement be rapid so that the time value can also make a contribution.

Usually the put and call volatilities are different, in which case the straddle value is given by a curve using the average of these volatilities. Figure 7–2 illustrates this point, where the circles give straddle values for a call volatility of 0.7 and a put volatility of 0.5 and are seen to fall on the curve for 0.6.

STRADDLE WRITING

You can open a position by selling a straddle. You expect the opposite conditions to those for its purchase. You look for a stock whose price is expected to remain near the striking price with narrow movement. You hope the options will expire when the stock price is at the striking price; so they will both be worthless. This is a pretty fine point, however, and you would be inclined to cover one or the other, or possibly both, rather than take a chance on exercise of an in-the-money option. Your profit is expected to be generated by the decreasing time values of both options. A price move in either direction from the striking price creates a potential loss. The move does not have to be very much to wipe out the credit of the sale, and it is unlimited in both directions. Straddle writing is a risky business if you guess wrong, and guessing right does not have much leeway.

The straddle writer is at all times faced with the risk of an exercise of the in-the-money option. This can fluctuate between the put and the call side. Margin is required on each option as if they were separate. The margin usually increases as the stock price moves in either direction from the striking price. With the possibility of the stock price moving from one side of the striking price to the other, it is possible that a straddle writer could receive exercise notices on both the puts and calls, that is, getting *whipsawed*. Better think twice before writing straddles.

PUT AND CALL COMBINATIONS

Selling the combination of a call at one striking price and a put at a lower striking price is of some interest. It has the feature of having zero value at expiration for any stock price between the striking prices (see Figure 7–3). This combination is less critical than selling a straddle, but the maximum profit is also less. You still have the problems of supplying margin and early exercise. This combination is suitable when you expect the stock to be fairly stable in price, depending on decreasing time values to provide a profit.

In a bull market, you might want to buy a call and sell a put, reducing your cash outlay to perhaps mere commission cost. If the stock price increases, you gain on both options. However, if the stock decreases, you lose on both options. The position requires margin on the short side. You could reverse the combination in a bear market, buying a put and selling a naked call.

Another combination is to combine puts and calls and expiration times. For example, what one might call a time straddle would be to

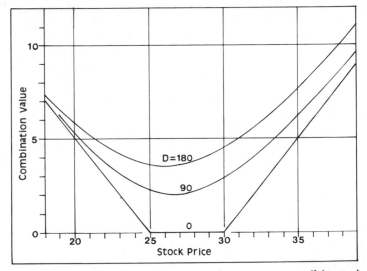

Figure 7–3.   Value of the combination of one put at a striking price of 25 and one call at the striking price of 30 when both options have a volatility of 0.6. This combination has the interesting feature of having zero value at expiration for any stock price between the two striking prices.

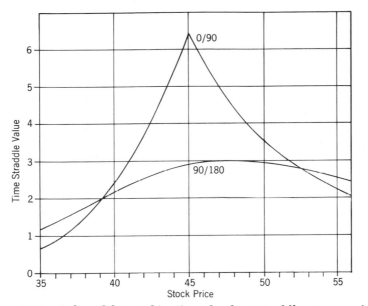

Figure 7–4.   Value of the combination of a short straddle at one expiration time and a long straddle at an expiration time 90 days later. All striking prices are 45, and the average of the put and call option volatility is 0.6.

sell a straddle at one expiration time and buy a straddle expiring at a later time, both at the same striking price. This combination is the same as a horizontal call spread with a horizontal put spread. Figure 7–4 shows the result for such a combination for a striking price of 45 and option volatility of 0.6, or an average of 0.6 for the put and call. The lower curve shows the net cost before commissions to buy a 180-day straddle and sell a 90-day straddle. The cost is about the same over a wide stock price range and might be about $300 for this example. At the time of expiration of the first to expire options, the value of the position is given by the upper curve, having a sharp maximum at the striking price. Although this curve lies above the cost curve over a wide price range, remember commissions have to be paid on perhaps as many as eight options. This could run to $100 per combination, depending on the number of contracts involved and the price of the individual options. The restricted price range coupled with the requirement that the stock price be in a narrow range at the particular time when the short option expires limits the profit potential. This is not a good strategy.

CONVERSIONS

Before straddles were traded in a secondary market, a technique was devised to convert puts to calls and calls to puts as a means to liquidate option positions. This was somewhat complex and is no longer necessary, since we have exchanged-traded options. The same result is obtained by a simple technique. If the holder of a straddle believes the stock has reached a high and is likely to reverse direction, he can sell his call and buy a put for less money. His call is converted to a put so that he now holds two puts. Conversely, if the stock falls to a low, at which he believes the price is likely to reverse direction, he could sell his put and buy a call. The conversion leaves him with two calls. This is like riding a roller coaster; it is a lot of fun if you can keep in phase with the oscillating stock price.

8 Miscellaneous

HEDGING

Hedging is entering into a second transaction to reduce risk in a first transaction. It is customarily the protection of a position in a common stock, either long or short, by taking an opposite position in options on this stock. The stock position may already have been taken at the time the hedge is established, or the two transactions may take place simultaneously. If you buy a stock at a price of 40, you can ensure that this stock can be sold at 40 by buying a put with a striking price of 40. This might cost you $400 and would allow you to put your stock to the seller of the put for a price of 40 any time up to the expiration date.

If you sold a stock short, you could hedge' by buying a call that would enable you to cover your short position at the striking price of the call, which eliminates the unlimited risk if the stock went up in price instead of down, as expected. The cost of the call is insurance against a large loss over the time until expiration of the call.

Hedging is more than the mere reduction of risk in a stock transaction. For example, you may own a stock in which you have a large paper profit, and you do not want to sell it; but you are concerned about the near-term prospects. You could buy a put that ensures that you could collect your profits, less the cost of the put, should the stock suffer reverses.

Protection can be obtained in reverse transactions to those described above, and such positions are likewise termed hedging. For example, you could own a stock and sell a call on it, which gives you protection against a small decrease in stock price; that is, you would have no loss until the decrease in stock value exceeded what you received for the call. This is covered writing; so no margin is required. If the stock does not move to a point above the striking price at expiration time, you pocket the sale proceeds of the call. If the call is exercised, you receive only the striking price for your stock no matter how high the market price. You took this chance, forgoing possible profits, when you sold the call to attain some downside protection.

HEDGE RATIO

You might sell two calls for each 100 shares of stock owned to give protection for a greater fall in stock price. One call would be covered writing, as discussed above. The other call would be written naked and requires margin. This may be extended to even more calls per 100 shares. The ratio of the calls written for each 100 shares of stock is called the *hedge ratio*. The greater the hedge ratio, the more the stock can fall in price before you have an overall loss on the position. If the position is held to expiration of the options, all their time value will have disappeared, and if the stock price has risen above the striking price, you will have a profit in the stock, but this will be reduced by the cost of covering the intrinsic value of the calls. There will be some point on the upside at which the gain in stock price just balances the loss on covering the short calls. This is the *upside break-even* point. The *downside break-even* point is where the loss in stock value just balances the money received on the sale of the calls. The actual break-even points must take commissions into account. The upper and lower break-even points may be adjusted relative to one another by varying the hedge ratio. You may desire to set them so that they are equally distant above and below the striking price, so as to give equal protection for stock price moves in either direction. Hedge ratios are customarily calculated for the time that the options expire when the option values are known in terms of the stock price and striking price.

ALTERNATIVE POSITIONS

We discussed buying a put as a hedge against loss in a long stock position. If the stock does go down, the loss is limited to the cost of the put plus commissions. There is the alternative of merely buying a call. Disregarding any differences in the price of a put and a call at the time, the loss for a fall in stock price is the same except you have fewer commissions to pay if buying only the call and your invested capital is much less. As to the upside potential, the call will be worth as much as the stock increases in price above the striking price, and selling it will cost less in commissions than selling the stock.

A similar situation exists in buying a call to protect a short stock position. Buying a put instead requires less invested capital, no margin, no dividends to pay on borrowed stock, and lower commissions but provides the same participation in the stock price movement.

All option positions have equivalent positions in terms of stock and other options. They are summarized in Table 8–1. These positions are strictly equivalent only if commissions, margin, and invested capital are disregarded. These factors may be the deciding factor on choice of strategy. The simple option positions, now available in exchange-traded options, allow us to do simply many things that had previously been done by more complicated methods.

Assume we are bullish on a stock and want to trade it. We could buy the stock, buy a call, or buy the alternative of a call, that is, purchase the stock and a put. Let us examine these alternatives. If buying the stock, considerably more capital is required, but this is not necessarily a problem. We have said that only a small part of one's funds should be committed to option trading and that a conservative program is to keep the bulk in some cash equivalent, producing nominal interest income. If instead, the funds are committed to common stock, often dividends are received that may offset the loss of interest. If the stock alone is purchased, it could go down in price by almost any amount; so you have a large risk. If instead, a call is purchased, the risk is limited to the cost of the call plus commissions, which is much less. The possible dollar gain is almost as much as could be obtained by trading the stock alone, but of course the percentage gain would be much greater. The call value will increase with the stock price, but since its time value decreases while you wait for the stock to advance in price, its dollar gain will be somewhat less than that of the stock; but commissions involved are less, which tends to balance out this difference.

The third alternative of buying the stock and a put reduces the risk and for some pricing conditions can produce the least risk of all. If the put is in the money and you exercise the put, you sell the stock for more

**Table 8–1. Equivalent Positions of
Options and Stock-Option Combinations**

Option Position	Option-Stock Equivalent
Long put	Short stock and long call
Long call	Long stock and long put
Short put	Long stock and short call
Short call	Short stock and short put
Long straddle	Short stock and long 2 calls, or long stock and long 2 puts
Short straddle	Long stock and short 2 calls, or short stock and short 2 puts

than you paid for it, and your loss, if having to close the position, is the maximum risk and can be specifically determined. As an example, Mesa Petroleum closed on June 9, 1977, at 32½ and its October 35 put at 3¼, the cost of the two being 35¾. If the price went against you, you could close your position by exercising the put for a loss of only ¾ point plus commissions. If you had purchased an October 35 call instead, your loss would have been $2^3/16$ points, the cost of the call plus commissions. Taking commissions into account and assuming 200 shares and the corresponding two option contracts, the loss on buying the stock and put would be $382, but the loss on buying two calls would be $470, a greater risk. As it turned out, the stock went up in price, and the position could have been closed out as follows:

Date	Stock Price	Oct 35 Put	Oct 35 Call	Stock and Put Gain	Call Gain
July 5	40¼	1	7⅛	$ 827	$ 938
July 22	46¾	¾	11⅝	1972	1795
Oct 20	39⅛	1/16	4	358	300

If the position is held only a short time, with a moderate increase in stock price, the call would have some time value and, as shown, would produce a greater profit. When the price moves up farther, the time value may vanish, and the stock-put combination produces a greater profit because the stock price increase is greater than the intrinsic value of the call.

The example above was for the intermediate-term options. At this time the shorter-term put was not offered, but it might have been considered too limited in time for the stock to increase as expected. The January options were available and could have been chosen, but the put was quoted at 4, thus increasing the risk. This might have been worthwhile if you were convinced that the stock would continue to increase in price for more than the approximate 4 months the October options had to go.

The stock-put combination could have been turned into an equivalent bullish vertical spread by selling an October 40 call at 7/16. This would cut the risk to 5/16 point before commissions, but it would place an upper limit on the possible gains if the stock price rose above 40. Above 40, the short call, which would have to be covered at expiration, would increase in price by the same amount as the stock increases in price for offsetting gain and loss. If opening with the January options, the value of the call sold would be greater, and likewise the cost of the put. Above a stock price of 40 there is no advantage in holding the position for a longer time. In general, you are better off using the shorter to intermediate expiration times and staying out of the spread.

Timing of opening the stock-put position is made less critical by the fact that as the stock price varies, the intrinsic value of the put changes by the same amount in the opposite direction.

TAX CONSIDERATIONS

When the underlying stock becomes involved with your option transaction, special tax considerations may apply. You should check the current tax laws to see which may apply to you. These are summarized in the prospectus of the Options Clearing Corporation and in various pamphlets put out by the option exchanges. In general, the option proceeds are combined with those of the stock, and the holding period of the stock may be affected.

Income tax laws frequently change; so you should keep abreast of the current situation. Also, tax laws are subject to interpretation that may vary from time to time, and at times there are questions as to how the IRS may rule on a specific situation. There are many aspects of taxes that apply to options and their related securities; it is advisable to avoid questionable situations. You should obtain current tax advice before entering into any transaction whose tax aspects may be in question. Some of the more common situations are summarized below for listed options; additional conditions may arise with unlisted options. More details may be found in books on taxes for investors and traders (see reference 4, Appendix E). The following comments are intended only to alert you to the various points to be considered, which you may want to investigate further.

Options are considered capital assets. The purchase price is considered an incomplete expenditure until the option is sold, exercised, or allowed to expire. If it is allowed to expire, it is considered to have been sold on the expiration date.

Since exchange-traded options have a life of no more than 9 months, gains and losses will be short-term under present law. The simple purchase and sale of an option without a position in the underlying security thus results in a short-term capital gain or loss.

If a put or call is purchased and later exercised, the cost of a call is added to the cost of the stock acquired, and the cost of a put is subtracted from the proceeds of the stock sold. The holding period of the stock obtained by exercise of a call begins on the day of exercise.

If you or your spouse own the underlying stock when a put is purchased, this may be treated as a short sale of the stock. If the stock has been held for less than 1 year, any gain realized on the sale of this stock, whether by closing the short sale by exercising the put or otherwise, will be short-term gain, even though the stock may have been held for more than 1 year when sold. If the put is sold, to close the option position, the damage has already been done, and the holding period of the stock is lost and does not start over until the put is sold. This applies only to the number of shares equivalent to the put purchased. If the stock has been held for more than 1 year when the put is purchased, the purchase of the put is not a short sale, and the holding period of the stock continues to run. Any loss on closing the position is considered a long-term loss.

There is an exception to the short-sale rule. If the put and stock are both purchased on the same day, the stock being identified as held for exercising the put and actually so used, the short-sale rule does not apply.

Wash sales can produce complex tax considerations. If an investor sells stock or securities at a loss and within a 30-day period before or after the sale acquires substantially identical securities, the loss is disallowed. This is known as a *wash sale*. The purchase of a call is considered to be a substantially identical security with its underlying stock. Though the loss is disallowed for this transaction, it is transferred to the new security. This may work to your advantage or disadvantage, depending on your tax position for the year. If you sell a security at a loss and within 30 days discover your timing was bad with respect to taking the loss, you could purchase a substantially identical security and add back the holding period and loss. If you own a stock with a short-term loss and wish to prevent the loss from becoming long-term, you could purchase a put that would wipe out the holding period, and it would not restart until the put is sold. If you hold a stock with a long-term loss, you could sell the stock and purchase its call, which would cause the loss to be disallowed and added to the basis of the call along with its holding period. If then the call is exercised, the new stock would include the basis of the call, but the holding period would disappear, and the stock could be sold, realizing a short-term loss. Remember the price paid for the call and the additional commissions reduce the possible tax gains. Tax manipulations such as these should be checked against current tax laws and interpretations before initiating the transaction.

If holding stock with a short-term gain, you could sell a call having an expiration date far enough in the future so that the stock holding period would be long-term. If the stock goes up in price beyond the striking price, you could wait for the exercise, or after the stock has gone long-term, you could close the option position and sell the stock. This would give you a long-term gain on the stock and a short-term loss on the call. Should the stock decrease in price, the sale of the call gives some protection while waiting for the long-term gains to mature. If the call sold is in the money, the chance of exercise is increased, and since the sale price is added to the sale price of the stock, this premium is likewise long-term gain.

9 Option Formulas

—Options from the mathematician's point of view

For effective use of options, one needs to know what is a reasonable price for the option of interest and how this price will vary with time and under different conditions. Mathematical formulas can be derived that take into account the various circumstances and provide a value that is representative or said to be a normal or average value. These formulas enable one to spot overvalued or undervalued option quoted prices, to predict the most likely price for an option at some future time under various assumed conditions, and to compare different options with respect to their probable price movements.

Two basic approaches are available for establishing the option formulas. One is to develop a theoretical model, the other to use the historical price data and fit an assumed equation to give a good fit to these data. The discussion that follows is presented for those who want to know more about the derivation of the formulas and who may want to explore similar investigations on their own. An understanding of this chapter is not necessary for successful trading in options. One needs only to use the final results in the form of the equations or the tables constructed from the formulas.

THEORETICAL MODELS

Most call formulas derived by the theoretical approach are based on the work of Black and Scholes.* You need to be a mathematician to understand these formulas, and a programmable calculator is essential to compute the call values. The model has wide acceptance and gives good results.

* Fischer Black and Myron Scholes. "Options and Liabilities." *Journal of Political Economy*, **81**, 637 (1973).

Texas Instruments developed a program based on the Black and Scholes model that they stored on a magnetic card for their SR-52 Programmable Slide-Rule Calculator; with these facilities you could make your own calculations. Their model includes the short-term interest rate in addition to the obvious factors of stock price, striking price, time to expiration, and volatility. Other factors may be introduced in theoretical models such as the dividend on the stock.

THE STATISTICAL APPROACH

In this book, we have used formulas based on making a statistical fit to the closing price quotations for the option and the stock under a wide variety of market conditions. One can assume various forms for the basic equations and adjust the constants to give a good fit to the historical data. One should not expect any one specific equation to be the correct form, but, instead, several forms could be used with perhaps comparable results. The formulas were chosen to be relatively simple and capable of understanding by one of only moderate mathematical knowledge. The computation can be carried out with the modest hand-held slide-rule calculators or even with pencil and paper, but if many computations are to be made, a programmable calculator is desirable.

CALL FORMULAS

The procedure used in arriving at the formula for exchange-traded calls will be described in some detail. This book confines its discussion to options on stocks, but the field of options is expanding to other investment vehicles, and the methods used here may be found useful for these other situations as well.

When the underlying stock is selling exactly at the option striking price, the price of the calls on this stock represents a pure time value. It is normal for this time value to be larger in magnitude as the time remaining to expiration is greater, hence a value proportional to time. A rule of thumb is that the time value of a call varies as the square root of the time remaining to expiration. This is only approximate, and we will derive a more exact formula.

As the underlying stock price increases above the striking price of the call, the call takes on additional value. The difference between the stock price and the striking price $(P - S)$ is frequently referred to as the *intrinsic value* of the call. It may be observed that the price of the call is not the sum of the time value, when $P = S$, and the intrinsic value but is a value somewhat less. Thus, our price formula has to take into account the interaction of these two aspects

We note also that the price of a call for a high-priced stock is greater than for a low-priced stock; in fact the call value is roughly proportional to the stock price, that is, it is some percentage of the stock price. Comparing different stocks, we note also some stocks consistently support a higher price for their calls than another stock at the same price, even though the expiration dates and striking prices are the same. This difference is related more or less directly to the stock volatility.

Our first assumption is that the value of a call O_c when the stock price P is at the striking price S may be given by

$$O_c = PAV \qquad\qquad (9\text{--}1)$$

where A is a function of the time until expiration only and V is a factor defined as the *option volatility*, which includes everything affecting the value of the call except stock price, striking price, and time to expiration.

The first step is to determine the equation for A. Based on our initial assumption that Equation (9–1) applies only when $P = S$, we search out those quotations in the daily closing prices in which this equality exists. Published data giving exact time relations between the call price and stock price are not available, and in fact the two executions may not take place at the same time or near the same time. The most readily available data are the closing prices on the options exchanges for calls and the stock exchange for the stock. Differences that may arise because of the closing call price's occurring at a different time from the closing stock price can be minimized by, first, selecting options that are actively traded and, second, averaging a large number of data points. We are endeavoring to find a value that is an average and so must use a large number of data points in any case. Any single data point may deviate from the average, because that option may be overvalued or undervalued.

There are other sources of data that may be used to select executions that are more closely related in time, but they may be impractical; the closing price data are readily available in the *Wall Street Journal* and other daily newspapers. One of these sources is one of the stock market quote systems that give the time of the last trade. Several quote systems have terminals that are available to the individual investor on a rental basis. Another is the "Fitch Sheets," which may be available to you through your broker or library. These list all transactions on the NYSE and AMEX for stocks by time in minute intervals, but the CBOE and AMEX options are listed only by hourly intervals (at present).

A second assumption is now made as to the equation for A, which could be that A equals the square root of D, where D is the time to expiration of the option. We express D in calendar days. With this added assumption we know all quantities in Equation (9–1) except V. There are generally three calls available for any one striking price. If our assumed equation is correct, we should obtain the same value when the equation is solved for V, that is, $V = O_c/PA$, for each of the three times to expiration. By tabulating a number of samples, we can quickly observe whether this is true. One should not expect exact agreement, for the quoted values fluctuate from normal. The first test is to note whether the value of V tends to increase or decrease when going from the near-term option to the intermediate-term and likewise when going from the intermediate-term to the last to expire. For a good fit, these differences should show as many decreases as increases. If not, the equation for A must be modified. One can break down the tabulation into a series of time to expiration intervals to give more specific detail of the desired function. Finally, our initial assumption was that the call value was directly proportional to the first power of the price. This can be tested by tabulating the data by price intervals. How much data are needed before obtaining a satisfactory answer? One should include enough to cover all types of market conditions; then by tabulating in steps, like 25 sets at a time, a time is reached at which the ratio of the total increases to the total decreases of V approaches unity. A small error in the equation accumulates a bias in one direction or the other, and it becomes obvious that something has to be changed. The resulting equation found by this process is

$$A = (\sqrt{D} + \ln \sqrt{D} + 0.013D - 1) \div 100 \qquad (9\text{--}2)$$

The division by 100 is merely to adjust the V values to eliminate the zeros following the decimal point (V values range from about 0.3 to 1.3). The symbol ln is the natural logarithm. The value of A is arbitrarily established as essentially zero for the day before expiration.

The next step is to introduce the variation between stock price and striking price. Whatever formulas we now choose must revert to Equation (9–1) when $P = S$. There are some other boundary conditions that must be met. The calls can never be negative in value but can be zero when the stock price falls sufficiently below the striking price. When the stock price rises above the striking price, the call must always have a value at least as great as the difference between the stock price and the striking price, even at expiration time. The out-of-the-money calls must decrease to zero at expiration. In-the-money calls have a component of value equal to $P - S$ that has been termed their intrinsic value. This component can be represented as a straight line on a stock price versus call value plot, going through the point $P = S$ at zero call price as represented by line AB in Figure 9–1. We know the call versus stock-price curve goes through the point $O_c = PAV$ for $P = S$. As it moves upward, it falls toward the line AB. For out-of-the-money calls, the curve must start at the point PAV and fall toward the zero axis. We assume exponential functions of the same form for both these curves and adjust the constants to fit the data. The formulas finally derived are

$$O_c = PAVe^{(P - S)/2PAV} \qquad\qquad P < S \qquad (9\text{--}3)$$

and

$$O_c = PAVe^{-(P - S)/2PAV} + (P - S) \qquad P > S \qquad (9\text{--}4)$$

The quantity e is the base of natural logarithms and equals 2.71828.

The constants of the equation were established by first using the data points used in establishing A to determine the value of V for calls of the specific stock and then computing the call values for all other available calls in the class. The deviations from quoted price are then found, and these differences were tabulated by stock price and striking price versus brackets of time to expiration and again versus volatility. Equalizing the plus and minus differences was accomplished by adjusting the constants of the formulas. Also, the way the calls varied as $P - S$ changed, when several striking prices were quoted, was examined for error trend.

We may ask, what does a normal value mean? In a sense, it is the average or expected value of the call for the fixed and determinable conditions of the underlying stock price and time to expiration for the particular call in question. The individual stock characteristics are introduced in the quantity V, which we have called option volatility, but it is more than this. It also takes account of general market conditions and other undeterminable factors, averaging them over the period of time used in establishing V. The individual option may deviate above or below the computed normal value. When these deviations persist, we may consider the normal value has changed, and we may want to redetermine V. The usefulness of the formulas for computing normal values does not lie in being able to predict precisely where in price the options will trade under specified conditions but lies in providing a reference value to which trading values may be referred to determine their relative values and deviations. No matter what option formula you may use, these deviations will occur, and it is hard to say just what is a

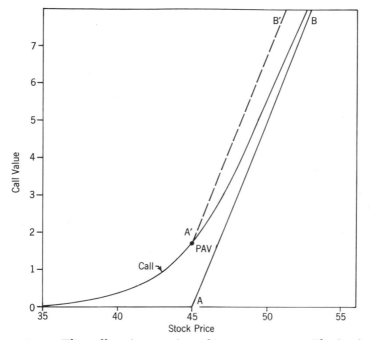

Figure 9–1. The call option consists of two components. The intrinsic value, represented by line *AB*, is given by $P - S$ for stock prices P above the striking price S and is zero for prices below the striking price. The other component, dependent on various factors, has a maximum when $P = S$, shown as point A', and decreases as the stock price moves away from the striking price.

normal value. When stock characteristics change, market conditions vary, etc.; your formula has to be updated. The updating required in Equations (9–3) and (9–4) involves only a redetermination of V; the other quantities are explicit. The formulation of Equations (9–3) and (9–4) has been established to meet the fixed boundary conditions of the market operation and to represent on a statistical basis the general movement of option values.

HOW THE FORMULAS WORK OUT

How well the formulas represent normal option values can be examined by comparing point by point the computed values with the quoted values, but there will be variations due to their normal deviation from normal values. A convincing demonstration is provided in Tables 9–1 to 9–3.

Table 9–1. Comparison of Computed Call Values

Comparison of computed call values with quoted prices for (1) a formula based on the theoretical model of Black and Scholes and (2) the statistical fit described in this book. The data are for August 9, 1974, near the end of a bear market, when the short-term interest rate was 12%. The DJIA closed at 77.30. Time to expiration was 77 days for the October call, 168 for January, 259 for April.

Stock and Price	S	V		October Call			January Call			April Call		
				Price	(1)	(2)	Price	(1)	(2)	Price	(1)	(2)
IBM	200	(1)	0.273	19¼	18.24	17.95	25¼	26.25	24.63	32¼	33.01	29.96
208½	220	(2)	0.607	9¼	7.84	8.43	15¼	15.54	14.97	20¼	22.19	20.23
	240			3½	2.86	3.92	8⅛	8.44	9.07			
	270			⅞	0.36	1.25						
EasKd	90	(1)	0.272	5¾	5.42	5.54	8¼	8.90	8.54	11	11.82	10.91
89⅝	100	(2)	0.583	2½	1.74	2.31	4¾	4.56	4.82	6½	7.22	6.95
	120			⅜	0.08	0.40						
Polar	25	(1)	0.739	4⅝	4.51	4.55	6¼	6.42	6.53	8⅝	7.88	8.10
26⅜	30	(2)	1.317	2½	2.48	2.36	3¾	4.47	4.25			
	35			1 3/16	1.30	1.22	2½	3.10	2.76			
	40			9/16	0.67	0.63	1 7/16	2.15	1.79			
	45			⅜	0.34	0.33	¾	1.49	1.17			
	60			3/16	0.04	0.05	⅜	0.52	0.32			
Gt Wst	10	(1)	0.625	1 5/16	1.49	1.53	2	2.16	2.23	2⅜	2.68	2.78
10⅜	15	(2)	1.172	7/16	0.20	0.23	⅞	0.68	0.65			
	20			⅛	0.02	0.04	⅜	0.21	0.19			

Table 9–2. Comparison of Computed Call Values

This table is similar to Table 9–1 except for the date of February 7, 1975, at the beginning of a bull market, when short-term interest rates were 6% and the DJIA closed at 711.91. The expiration times for the three calls are the same as in Table 9–1.

Stock and Price	S	V	April Call Price	(1)	(2)	July Call Price	(1)	(2)	October Call Price	(1)	(2)
IBM	160	(1) 0.300	39½	40.17	40.09	44½	44.09	44.09	46¼	47.91	47.88
197⅝	180	(2) 0.551	23½	23.16	23.32	29	28.95	28.83	33½	33.78	33.42
	200		11³/₈	10.93	10.79	17³/₈	17.48	17.04	21³/₈	22.70	21.97
	220		5⅛	4.17	4.66						
EasKd	60	(1) 0.237	18¼	19.27	18.92	18¼	20.27	19.91	17½	21.34	20.96
78½	70	(2) 0.475	9⅝	9.86	9.94	11½	11.62	11.65	12⅝	13.19	13.13
	80		3¾	3.18	3.40	6¼	5.36	5.52			
	90		1⁵/₁₆	0.58	1.00						
	100		³/₁₆	0.06	0.29						
Polar	15	(1) 0.627	6	6.12	6.41	6¾	6.89	7.40	7½	7.56	8.28
20⅝	20	(2) 1.091	2⅞	2.78	2.79	4	3.99	4.08	4½	4.91	5.10
	25		1¼	1.05	1.01	2¼	2.21	2.10			
Gt Wst	10	(1) 0.518	5⅜	5.29	5.40	5⅞	5.61	5.88			
15⅛	15	(2) 0.908	1⁹/₁₆	1.58	1.57	2⅜	2.35	2.36	3	2.94	2.98

Table 9–3. Comparison of Computed Call Values

These values are for January 30, 1976, when the market was rising strongly and the short-term interest rate was 4.75%. The DJIA closed at 975.28. Times to expiration are the same as in the two previous tables.

Stock and Price	S	V	April Call Price	(1)	(2)	July Call Price	(1)	(2)	October Call Price	(1)	(2)
IBM 257³/₄	180		78¹/₂	79.52	78.22						
	200	(1) 0.226	58⁵/₈	59.76	58.83	60¹/₂	62.57	61.60			
		(2) 0.428									
	220		38⁷/₈	40.44	40.24	43³/₄	44.63	44.27	47¹/₄	48.68	48.22
	240		25⁵/₈	23.25	23.47	28	29.21	29.14	33¹/₈	34.17	33.79
	260		10³/₄	10.76	10.92	16¹/₂	17.39	17.34	21	22.65	22.33
EasKd 113	90	(1) 0.290	24¹/₄	24.08	24.14	26¹/₂	25.90	26.23			
	100	(2) 0.535	16	15.15	15.44	18¹/₂	17.95	18.31			
	110		8⁵/₈	8.12	8.23	11¹/₄	11.60	11.71	14	14.31	14.42
	120		4¹/₂	3.64	3.86	6⁵/₈	6.99	7.14	8³/₈	9.69	9.78
Polar 37³/₄	30	(1) 0.487	8⁷/₈	8.58	8.89	10¹/₄	9.80	10.34	11¹/₈	10.86	11.60
	35	(2) 0.848	5¹/₈	4.98	5.09	6¹/₂	6.68	6.89	7¹/₂	7.97	8.30
	40		2¹⁵/₁₆	2.57	2.52	4¹/₄	4.38	4.33			
Gt Wst 16³/₄	10	(1) 0.460	7	6.85	6.89	6¹/₂	7.03	7.24			
	15	(2) 0.794	2⁷/₁₆	2.48	2.54	3	3.16	3.25	3¹/₂	3.69	3.82
	20		¹¹/₁₆	0.46	0.47	1¹/₄	1.11	1.07	1¹/₂	1.66	1.59

These tables compare the computed call values with the quoted price for a wide range of parameters. Also, the formulas we derived are compared with the Black and Scholes model as programmed by Texas Instruments for their SR-52 programmable calculator.

The three tables are for times of very different market conditions. Table 9–1, for closing prices as of August 9, 1974, is near the end of a bear market with 12% short-term interest rate. Table 9–2, for February 7, 1975, is at the beginning of a bull market with interest rate of 6%. Table 9–3, for January 30, 1976, is for a strongly rising market with low interest rate of 4.75%.

The same four stocks were selected for each table. They represent the full range of stock prices from the highest to lowest. Their volatilities vary over more than a two-to-one range. These particular choices, at these times, had an unusually large number of striking prices available. These wide ranges of conditions provide a good illustration of how well the formulas may be expected to provide useful values or how the calls may be over- or undervalued. On this point, remember the closing price of the stock and call may not be at the same time, which could give rise to some of the differences.

The volatilities for both formulas were found by substituting values in the formula until the computed call value agreed with the quoted value for each of the calls at the option striking price nearest above and below the stock price, when available, and taking their average to use in computing all the values in the tables. The Black and Scholes formula also uses the short-term interest rate, but its value is not critical, as errors are compensated for by adjusting the value of the volatility. Equations (9–3) and (9–4) include the effect of interest rates and all other quantities, other than price and time, in the volatility factor. No comparison should be made between volatility values of the two formulas, as they do not enter the formulas in the same way.

PUT FORMULAS

When puts started trading on the exchanges, the formulas derived for calls were tested against the put quotations, taking into account the inverse relationship between puts and calls. The option volatility for each option of the entire class of put options was computed, and the values were found to be consistant with respect to both striking prices and times to expiration. The same computations were made for the corresponding calls. The volatilities were averaged and the standard deviations determined. It was found that the standard deviations for

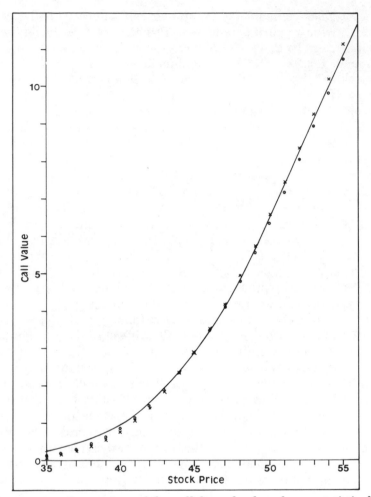

Figure 9–2. Comparison of the call formulas based on a statistical fit (solid curve) with a theoretical model using short-term interest rates of 5% (○'s) and 10% (×'s). The values are normalized to give the same call value at the point at which the stock price is at the striking price (45).

put and call volatilities were essentially the same. The volatilities do vary between puts and calls, depending on the individual stock.

The complete set of option formulas can be written as follows:

$$O_c = T \qquad\qquad P < S \qquad\qquad (9\text{--}5)$$

$$O_c = T + (P - S) \qquad P > S \qquad\qquad (9\text{--}6)$$

$$O_p = T + (S - P) \qquad P < S \qquad\qquad (9\text{--}7)$$

$$O_p = T \qquad\qquad P > S \qquad\qquad (9\text{--}8)$$

where O_c is the call option value, O_p the put option value, and T the time value for either and given by

$$T = PAVe^{-|P - S|/2PAV} \qquad\qquad (9\text{--}9)$$

EFFECT OF INTEREST RATE

Figure 9–2 gives the plotted curve for Equations (9–3) and (9–4) for the striking price of 45. The plotted circles give the computed values of calls using the Black and Scholes model, as programmed for the SR-52, and using a short-term interest rate of 5%. The volatilities were adjusted to give identical values when the striking price and stock price are equal. The theoretical model gives slightly lower values as the stock price moves away from the striking price. The points plotted as X's are for a 10% short-term interest rate with the volatility adjusted to give the same call value when the stock price is at the striking price. Even for a doubling of interest rate, the computed values are not much different. For in-the-money calls, the points for the two interest rates fall to either side of the statistical curve. The volatility had to be decreased from 0.30 to 0.27 to compensate for the change of interest rate from 5 to 10%.

10 Timing, Indicators and Signals

—Understanding what the market is saying

In option trading, timing is of utmost importance. You must learn to predict the price movement of the underlying stock both as to time and extent if you are to beat the game. Market averages merely reflect what most stocks are doing; so knowing what the average is going to do is very helpful in picking times for favorable movement of individual stocks. We describe techniques for predicting the market as a whole and tracking individual stocks.

ATTITUDE

If you are to be good at timing, you must get into the proper frame of mind. In other words you must understand how psychology works on you and others and learn not to be influenced by what you hear and read but stick to what the indicators say rather than what you would like to hear or what others might be saying. You must learn that you yourself have a hard time to put aside what you would like to have happen and what others would like to see happen and therefore put forth as predictions rather than stick with the cold facts. It is a natural human reaction to put off action, convincing yourself that you can get a better selling price or a lower buying price if you wait a little longer.

Do not pay attention to the daily market comments you hear on the news wrap-up. These commentators always have an explanation for what the market did today. You can almost always find both good and bad news; so just pick the appropriate item, and you have a logical explanation for what happened. The comments almost always seem to be very knowledgeable but in fact have little bearing on the market timing. Sure, there are many times when the market reacts to specific

106

news events, but a deeper look would have shown that the market was going to move in this manner no matter what the news. The news merely triggers that which was going to happen. Sometimes the market is not ready to be triggered and fails to respond as one might expect. The commentators have the solution for this one, too. The market had anticipated the event. You cannot lose at this game. Listen to as much of this as you please for your amusement, but base your market timing on more solid ground.

SHORT TIME VERSUS LONG TIME

Timing can be divided into long term and short term and intermediate in between. The division lines are not well defined, but for our purpose we are primarily concerned with the short term, which corresponds to exchange-traded option durations. It is useful to know what the longer-term market trends are, for you are always better off to follow those strategies which go with the market trend. The longest-term movement that we need to consider is that which gives rise to what gets designated as bull and bear markets. They are well enough defined when they are past, but arguments abound over what kind of a market we are in most of the time during the current market. Again a lot of the argument seems to be based on what one hopes for rather than what the market is saying. The market and individual stocks move not only in bull and bear market cycles but also in many cycles of shorter duration. The bull and bear cycles are easy to see in any longer-term price plot of any stock market average. The lows are most pronounced, and you can see that they occur about every 4 years plus or minus some months.

CYCLIC THINKING

For a long time market technicans have had some appreciation of cyclic movements. For example, bull and bear movements, phases, legs, etc., are terms that assoicate with cycles. You must learn how to identify the various market cycles; then you will be in a position to predict price movements with considerable success.

If you are familiar with periodic motions in which the variable goes through a fixed cycle, repeatable cycle after cycle, having the same length or duration and a constant amplitude or swing, you must put this exact picture aside when thinking of stock price movements. When we speak of cyclic movements in stocks, we do not mean or expect them to be periodic; they are not exactly repeatable. Instead, the cyclic motion varies in duration from cycle to cycle and likewise in amplitude or price swing. You must not allow these variations to lead to disbelief in the cyclic theory, which has become more widely followed in recent years. For more extensive treatment of market cycles you are referred to references 1 and 2. What is important to know is that prices tend to move up and down in a pattern that does not change abruptly except on rare occasion. Some stocks at times follow a more consistant pattern than others. The patterns are more irregular and more difficult to identify in some stocks at times; but this need not concern you, for there are always enough that show clear patterns to take care of your trading needs.

The price patterns are found in price plots, preferably a high-low plot versus time. Daily plots are needed for the shorter cycles, and weekly plots for the longer cycles. Having found an interesting cyclic pattern, you need to know that the chances for this pattern to continue are much greater than 50 : 50. Further, if the length of the last cycle, or half-cycle, which can also be identified, differs from the previous cycle length, the chances are that the oncoming cycle will continue this change; that is, there is a tendency for the cycles to get longer when this is their past behavior or shorter if that is their recent history. Similar behavior applies to the magnitude of their price swings. Further, there is a tendency for the swings to be greater, the longer the duration, and vice versa. Understanding how these variations behave and knowing that sudden changes seldom occur, we can predict future price movement both as to time and price value.

TECHNICAL INDICATORS

The technician believes that the market itself is telling where we are, where we are going, and when. The fundamental approach to the stock market is based on an evaluation of the present and future worth of the company and how these values are reflected in the price of its stock. These valuations are basically long-term and do not tell you how the stock price is going to change over the short term. Because options have short lives, we must know how the stock is going to move over the short term and rather precisely when it should make its move. Therefore, the option trader must be a technician and follow proper technical indicators.

Technical indicators have been around for a long time, and additional ones continue to be added to the list. The picture can be pretty confusing. Many a market analyst has his own variation that he swears by. Others follow many indicators and try to come up with some general conclusion. The proponents of an indicator can make a convincing story in terms of history, but too often when you try to follow them in real time, it is difficult to come to a decision. Many indicators are made more complicated than necessary. It is probably unintentional, as market technicians stumble onto something which, for a time at least, appears to vary with the price movement. One very common type of indicator is a coincident one; that is, it agrees with the price movement, reaching its peak with the price peak, etc. This may appear good, but stop a minute; it tells you nothing that price does not tell you, and price is what you are interested in; so just watch the price, it is much simpler, and there is no hocus-pocus. If we confine our indicators to the basic elements of the market, the number becomes quite limited but covers all that the market is saying. Much of the confusion disappears, and we can easily understand the market language. There are other utterances from the marketplace coming from people as a group, the people that cause the market to do what it is doing. This can be informative if different groups can be identified, if they can be depended on to act in a consistant manner, and if we know what their response is under the various situations. Indicators based on group action tend to be longer-term than is desired for option trading, and, also, often the data are delayed in being available. This leaves us with that which shows on the tape day by day as the most useful data for our indicators. This boils down to price, volume, and breadth (the behavior of the majority of stocks), and their interactions.

PRICE—THE NUMBER ONE INDICATOR

The price movement of a stock or a market average is the most informative of all indicators. It tells us both how much and when. You need to chart the high-low daily price range to be able to see what price is saying (see Figure 10–1 as an example of this type of chart). This is a chart of the Dow Jones Industrial Average (DJIA) for January and February 1977. We must again make a point with respect to the evening news. Invariably we hear how many points the DJIA went up or down on the day. If it goes up 10 points, it sounds bullish. If it goes down 10 points, we get a bearish reaction. This can be very misleading; so again it is something to ignore. Go to your high-low chart to see what the market is doing. It is clear that the DJIA is in a steady downtrend during January 1977, but see, for example, days marked a and b in Figure 10–1.

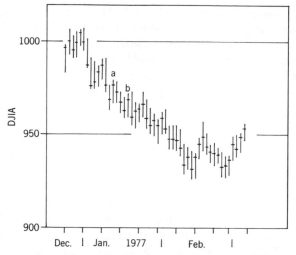

Figure 10–1. The daily high-low-close chart for the DJIA during January and February 1977 illustrates how the prices move in a rather well-defined channel and how the closing price can differ from the previous closing price by a considerable amount without the price movement getting out of the channel.

These are days when the market rose a considerable amount on the day, but it meant nothing. When these high-low bars are viewed with those before and after, they merely fit into the steady down trend pattern. This average has its very short cycles, 3 to 5 days here, and the timing was merely such that the average was near the high of the cycle when trading stopped for the day. You can use the information that when the market price starts a move late in the day, this move is most likely to continue on the next day's opening.

You may question what average to use. There are many, each having its own characteristics that someone believes to be better than the others. You hear many arguments on the advantages of one and deficiencies of another. For short-term purposes it makes very little difference, provided you can obtain the daily high and low and it is fairly broad-based, that is, not just one industry. We choose the DJIA because it is so generally available. Newspapers publish only closing prices for many of the other averages, and we have seen that this is not enough.

When the daily range is plotted, as in Figure 10–1, we see highs and lows tend to follow a more or less smooth upper and lower boundary. We used to call this a *channel* or *trend channel* and draw straight parallel lines through the upper and lower end points. With the more recent appreciation of the cyclic nature of stock price movements, these parallel lines are. allowed to be curved and follow the prices around maxima and minima. This "envelope" technique was first presented in detail by Hurst in reference 2. This envelope, consisting of two curved lines having a fixed vertical separation and touching the highs on one side and lows on the other, is easily drawn using a pair of dividers or a piece of paper marked with the vertical separation. Having drawn the envelope, we can see that it varies up and down and in fact describes a cyclic motion.

More than one envelope can be drawn. The one bounding the daily highs and lows has the smallest vertical separation, but you can draw another that bounds the maxima and minima of the first envelope (see Figure 10–2 as an example). With more compressed time scales, you can draw still other envelopes with greater vertical separation between their boundaries. These envelopes aid you in identifying price cyclic patterns. First, they designate points at which the price comes to the envelope boundary and then recedes. These successive points signify the bottom of successive cycles, when looking at the lower boundary, or the tops at the upper boundary. The time separations then give the cycle length. When you have a consistent pattern of cycles, you can be almost certain that another cycle will follow whose length is near the average of those just passed. Here is your price indicator making its prediction as to when the next low or high, as the case may be, will occur. Further, the envelope lines may be extended, following the past cyclic curvature, and you may expect the price movement to stop when it reaches the boundary of the extended envelope. Now, the price indicator is predicting how far the move will go. This indicator works for the small-

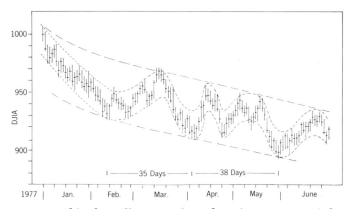

Figure 10–2.   This chart illustrates how the price movement is bounded by curved lines, known as price envelopes, that bring out the cyclic movement of prices.

est cycles, which last only a few days, to the longer ones, which are defined by the boundaries on the maxima and minima of the next smaller envelope, etc.

After some practice, you will see the high and low points that mark the cyclic top and bottoms without drawing the envelope. The bottoms tend to be better defined. You will want to mark these points on your chart, and you will want to distinguish between the cycles of different length. Frequently two or more cycles reach their extreme price movement at the same time. This leads to a more pronounced point. At other times, a short cycle may be almost exactly out of step or phase with a longer cycle and will flatten the peak of the longer cycle, thus obscuring this point or even producing the double top or bottom effect so often encountered. The true peak of the longer cycle may be between two small peaks. Watching for these occurences will avoid some confusion when at times your cycle seems to have missed its extreme position.

You often hear of testing the bottom or failing to exceed at the top. These expressions are nothing more than a recognition of the cyclic positions of the price movement. When the previous top or bottom holds and is not exceeded, it merely means the cycle has started rounding over and the price has reversed direction.

MOVING AVERAGES

If you know the closing price of a stock for each of 10 successive days, the average price for this 10-day period is found by adding the ten price values and dividing by the number of values (ten). This gives you a value representative of this 10-day period, and if you are plotting the price, this point would be located at the center of the 10-day period, which would for this example be between the fifth and sixth day. Now if you learn the price for the eleventh day, you can sum the last 10 days and divide by 10 to get a new 10-day average. It would be plotted at the center of the data span or 1 day later than the first point. As each new price on following days becomes available, you could repeat the procedure and move along in time 1 day at a time. This gives rise to the expression *moving average*. The prices normally have minor fluctuations that you would often like to smooth out. The moving average does just this. This is helpful in bringing out the price movement of interest and thus is an aid in making more apparent the cyclic picture. What we have described is the moving average as used by mathematicians to smooth data of all sorts. This is our purpose, and we are still talking about our price indicator, not a moving average indicator. The moving average is used in a different way by some as a market indicator, and most stock market publications, particularly stock charts, show various moving average curves for this purpose. These are something else for you to ignore, as they will not help you in developing your price indicator. The significant difference is where in time the value is plotted. You note, we plotted the average value at the center of the data span, and it is often referred to as a *centered moving average*. The other method is to plot the average at the time of the last data point. This gives a distortion and does not give you a curve following the average values of price. Various rules of interpretation are set forth to derive market indicators from this sort of plot, but not only is nothing new added, the picture is confused. You are much better off using price alone or its true representation—the centered moving average.

The moving average is in reality a filter that filters out or removes the minor fluctuations. What is minor is related to certain characteristics of the moving average. We have used 10 days, in our example, whose prices are averaged. This is known as a 10-day moving average and the *span* is the number of days that are summed. We can choose any number of days for the span. The larger the number of days, the greater the price smoothing. If the moving average were perfect in its filtering action, it would eliminate all price movements whose durations were less than the span and not affect those whose durations were longer than the span. It is not perfect; so it merely suppresses to some extent those cycles shorter than the span and passes only a part of the price swings that are longer than the span. The farther removed the cycle durations are from the span duration, the nearer the moving average approaches perfection. This imperfection affects only the amplitude of the price swings; the timing information is not altered. There is one further shortcoming to the moving average; it is that there is a delay in providing information. The plotted point, being at the center of the data span, only allows you to draw the moving average curve to the point one-half the span duration prior to the last day used in the data span. When you use long span lengths, this gets to be a problem. A more detailed discussion and methods for handling this problem may be found in Chapters 7 and 8 of reference 1.

There are some tricks in computing moving averages that save you a lot of time. It is useful to keep a plot of several span lengths on a chart with a market index. I prefer to plot the average of the daily high and low of the DJIA, with its 10-day, 30-day, and 60-day moving averages. You need to maintain a table that gives the date, the average of the high and low of the DJIA, the three moving average sums, and the corresponding moving averages, and also for easy reference a day number that merely keeps track of the number of market days from some zero reference date. You first compute the 10-day moving average. After getting your first value, the next value is found by merely adding the number for the new day to the previous 10-day sum and subtracting the oldest day's value. Since it is a 10-day average, division is accomplished by merely moving the decimal point. You can save time and avoid errors by cutting a card which just covers nine lines of your tabulation (you need ruled paper and preferably narrow ruled) and which you place over the last nine lines of daily prices used in the last sum. This locates the oldest day to be subtracted directly above the card, with the new day to be added being directly below the card.

The other spans are derived from the 10-day average. Again, take a card and mark the location of three lines spaced ten lines apart. Use this to locate three of the 10-day moving average values that you add and divide by 3 to obtain a 30-day moving average. In a similar manner use a card with two marks, separated by thirty lines, that locates two values of the 30-day moving average that are added and, when divided by 2, gives the 60-day moving average. The moving averages are plotted, with reference to the daily price plot, as follows: the 10-day one is plotted between the fifth and sixth prior days; the 30-day one between the fifteenth and sixteenth prior days; and the 60-day one between the thirtieth and thirty-first prior days. Check your plotting, from time to time, by counting back from the current day on your chart, 5 days, 15 days, and 30 days, which should be just ahead of the last plotted points.

These three moving averages are sufficient for the short-term market movements, but should you become interested in longer-term movements, the system may be extended to other spans that are multiples of an existing span. If longer than 60 days, it is better to go to a weekly plot, using the Friday value as the weekly value and calling the 60-day moving average a 13-week average (or 3-month average).

FINDING CYCLES FROM MOVING AVERAGES

Figure 10–3 shows the plot of the DJIA (average of daily high and low) and the three moving averages we have been discussing. Remembering that the moving averages serve as a filter, the 10-day average eliminates the very short fluctuations but contains all longer cycle components. The 30-day average tends to eliminate any additional cycles whose durations lie between 10 and 30 market days. Likewise, the 60-day average tends to eliminate additional cycles longer than 30 days but less than 60 days. This filtering action leads to the averages crossing

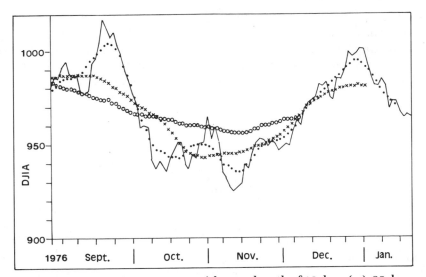

Figure 10–3.   Moving averages with span length of 10 days (...), 30 days (× × ×), and 60 days (○○○), plotted with price, show up the cyclic price movements.

over at various points that are ideally at the midpoints of the upswings and downswings. These points are one-half the cycle duration apart. These moving averages very often reveal the cyclic components of the price movement. Figure 10–3 illustrates this effect. These cycles stand out with greater prominence at the tops and bottoms of long cycles. The short cycles tend to be swamped by any rapid long-term swing.

VOLUME

Volume is a useful market indicator. It is a basic factor along with price. It is, however, interpreted as an adjunct to price movement. The normal behavior is for volume to be "in gear" with the price movement; that is, in a bullish market we expect volume to increase as prices increase and to dry up as prices retreat. In a bearish market the opposite is found; the volume increases as prices fall but dries up as prices increase. The indication comes about when the normal relationship fails. You can watch this on a very short-term basis, even hour by hour, to keep close track of market sentiment. Longer trends can be checked to indicate forthcoming turning points. You will need to average the daily volume figures. The moving average previously described can be used, or you can generally "eyeball" the conventional volume plot where the number of shares traded are represented by a vertical line.

Volume is a useful indicator when applied to individual stocks. When volume builds up greater than its past average, this is a sign of greater activity and makes the stock well worth watching.

BREADTH

Our third and final basic indicator is breadth, which measures the participation of all stocks in the market. It is measured in terms of the number of stocks advancing for the day and the number declining. There are various ways to combine these numbers, but for purposes of a short-term trading indicator we will adopt a form that provides an oscillator measuring what is called the overbought or oversold condition of the market. This is accomplished by subtracting the number of stocks declining from the number of stocks advancing. Various groups of stocks may be used, but we will use those of the New York Stock Exchange. This quantity fluctuates from day to day; so we need to smooth the values with a short-span moving average. Longer spans are sometimes used to bring out longer trends, but we can do well, for our purpose, with a 10-day moving average.

A modification of the true moving average, which was previously described, is useful where we are interested only in the change and do not need to relate to the input numbers. In this type of indicator we are looking for changes from the recent values. The new computed value can be materially affected by the oldest day, which is subtracted from the sum, if it is an unusually large or small value. This is known as the *drop-off* error. We are more interested in the newest data rather than this oldest day. We can make a modification that will reduce the weight of this old day by subtracting the average value instead of the oldest value. This modification has one other advantage, and this is that errors in arithmetic will be smoothed out with time and have no lasting effect, but errors in computing the true average can build up a permanent bias.

Our overbought-oversold indicator will be a 10-day modified moving average of the difference between the number of stocks advancing and the number declining each day on the NYSE. It will be plotted coincident with the current date. The 5-day delay is partly offset by the modification. This indicator moves between positive and negative values and at zero is considered neutral. It gives a cyclic pattern and tends to move rapidly from one extreme to the other.

When this indicator is well into the positive region, the market is said to be *overbought,* and when in the negative region *oversold.* The deeper it moves from neutral, the greater the expectations for a reversal. We use this indicator as an early warning, giving its signal when the reversal starts. This warning frequently comes ahead of the actual buy and sell points in the market. It does not work well alone, as you get too many whipsaws. It can be analyzed by drawing trend lines, which are broken by exceeding previous reactions and by a reverse movement greater than normal.

INTERACTIONS

Price, volume, and breadth form the basic vocabulary of the tape. We have discussed the meaning of each word and how to understand this simple language. As in any language, words can be put together to give further meanings. We want to examine what further the market can say with these three little words.

The number of shares traded is broken down between the number that exchanged hands at a price higher than the last price (*uptick*) and the number exchanging hands at a price lower than the last price (*downtick*). The daily financial data include figures on the *upside volume* and *downside volume* for the major exchanges. If the upside volume is greater than the downside volume, it is bullish. The reverse is bearish. It is very informative to chart these two volumes. The short fluctuations should be smoothed out, and a 10-day modified moving average is a good choice. These two moving averages should be plotted on the same coordinates, which then show not only their magnitude but their relative magnitude and their trend changes. When the upside-volume average lies well above the downside curve, it is bullish, and the reverse is bearish. The curves will cross over at points when the volume is changing from bullish to bearish, and vice versa. Further, trend changes give warning of a pending crossover. At times the two curves will be essentially in balance, indicating a neutral condition. A change will be indicated by a divergence developing between the two curves. Trend changes should last for at least 3 days to be significant. To use the upside-downside volume as an indicator, a signal can be considered as given when the curves move from a widely separated condition toward a crossover. Two criteria should be applied: one, that the trend changes should exist for at least 3 days; the other, the curves should move to within 150 million shares for the NYSE.

There is another combination of the basic data that is effective in making very short-term market predictions. It is obvious that if more stocks advance than decline on the day, it is a bullish indication. This can be measured by the ratio of advances to declines (A/D). Likewise, it is obvious that when the upside volume exceeds the downside volume, this is also bullish. It may be measured by the ratio of upside to downside volumes (u/d). Usually these two ratios move in the same direction; that is, both are greater than 1 in bullish markets, less than 1 in bearish markets. But we can get more than this from the numbers. We can ask if the stocks advancing are getting their fair share of the volume, more than their share, or less. This is done by taking the ratio of the two ratios already defined and is known as the *trading index*.* It is defined as $I = A/D \div u/d$. When I is less than unity, the advancing stocks are getting more than their normal volume, and it is a bullish indication. An I greater than 1 is a bearish indication.

If we look simultaneously at all three of the ratios, A/D, u/d, and I, we can form a composite index, the *three ratios index*, which will be termed bullish when all three ratios are bullish and bearish when all are bearish. Any other combination, including $I = 1$, is termed neutral. The three ratios index is a good indicator of the direction the market average will move within the next 2 days.

MARKET BUY AND SELL SIGNALS

Your buy and sell orders should be based on signals generated by the individual stock, but you will be better off if they are confirmed by the market as a whole. You will then be going with the trend. Some stocks do move contrary to the average, like golds at times, but be sure of your ground if you choose to buck the trend. Often the individual stocks will give their signal ahead of, or later than, the market average by a few days. There is a tendency for this difference to be repeatable. These variations are to be expected, for the market tells only what the average stock is doing. This is not very troublesome, for you have warnings of the market signals before the actual signal is produced by the mechanical methods we will presently describe.

The elements that are put together to form market buy and sell signals have already been discussed in the section on indicators. Our discussion is confined to signals for short-term trading as is appropriate to the option market. The first thing to do is to establish the cyclic position and pick out the cycle duration you want to use as your trading

---

* Richard W. Arms, Jr. "Jack be Nimble." *Barron's*, Aug. 7, 1967, p. 5.

cycle. We have seen that the market exhibits cycles from a few days in length upward. Ordinarily you would look for a trading cycle of at least a few weeks to as much as a couple of months. It must be long enough for the stock movement to produce a good option profit after commissions. Having picked your trading cycle, you can predict the approximate time for the next low or high as the case may be. The signal will be pinpointed by reference to market indicators. These indicators will at times give a signal or almost develop a signal that you will want to ignore. You ignore it if it does not come at a time when a signal should be expected from the cyclic position of the trading cycle you have chosen. If it agrees with the cyclic position, you act at once.

The pinpointed signal is developed as follows. First the overbought-oversold indicator will signal a reversal. This one indicator requires some subjective judgement. You decide on the basis of breaking a trend line, a divergence with the price trend, exceeding a previous reaction or a strong reversal move. It sometimes breaks a trend line in a flat or rounding over action only to pull back to try again. If the pullback exceeds the previous turning point, consider the signal canceled, and start all over. Usually when the true signal comes, the movement is swift enough so that there is no question. This signal is used only as a warning to watch for the more precise signals of other indicators, but the final signal is never generated unless there is the confirming overbought-oversold signal, which can, on occasions, occur on the same day as all other signals but usually precedes them.

Next, the upside-downside volume curves must indicate a reversal by moving toward a crossover or diverging out of a neutral condition. Their change of trend must have held for at least 3 days and, when moving from a widely separated condition toward a crossover, have approached to within 150 million shares when using the NYSE data. The final criterion is for the three ratios index to signal a market movement in the appropriate direction. You will ordinarily obtain these data after the market closes for the day. Orders can be placed on the following day. Remember not to mark a signal for your purpose unless it occurs at a time corresponding to the trading cycle you have chosen; otherwise, you will most likely be whipsawed. Figure 10–4 illustrates the development of the market buy and sell signals.

STOCK SIGNALS

The buy and sell signals as applied to individual stocks are used to initiate your market transactions. They will be based on price action

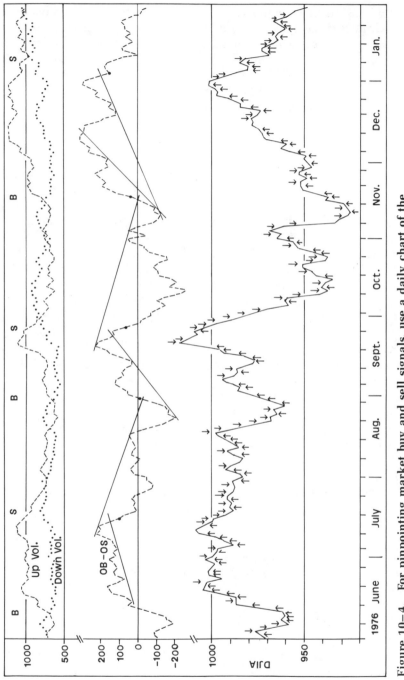

Figure 10–4. For pinpointing market buy and sell signals, use a daily chart of the average of the high and low values for the DJIA, a 10-day modified moving average of the difference between number of stocks advancing and declining (OB-OS), and the 10-day modified moving averages of the upside (---) and downside (...) volumes. The three ratios index is indicated by arrows.

alone, but within the framework of the cyclic representation and general market action. One important point is that stocks will produce both buy and sell signals whether in an uptrend or downtrend. You should enter a transaction only when your strategy enables you to go with the trend.

You must have a daily high-low chart of the stocks you are interested in, and they should be producing clear cyclic patterns. The approximate buy and sell times are estimated from the projected cycle. After a signal has been given, the ideal price pattern will round over as it changes direction, and minor cycles of price reactions will produce maxima when the trend is down and minima in uptrends. Successive reactions should be connected by a straight trend line. As the price movement continues, the trend becomes steeper, and new maxima or minima are produced. You redraw the trend line to give the steepest trend. Eventually, near the projected next cyclic turning point, the trend line is broken by the price reaction. This is the signal for price reversal. Examples are shown in Figure 10–5.

A useful technique for studying stock price movements is a transparent overlay on which you have traced the curve of a daily market average. When this is placed over your stock chart and dates brought into register, the stock price movement can be studied relative to the market. You can see whether your stock is stronger or weaker than the market, whether its cycles follow the market, and, by moving it back and forth in time, whether its price tends to lead or follow the market oscillations. You must use the same time scale for both the stock charts and the market average. You do not need to try to match the price scales; if they are chosen to be contained on the same size of chart paper, this will suffice. A scale of 50 DJIA points to the inch versus 2½ points to the inch for the medium-priced stock is found to be satisfactory.

When closing a position in which you have a gain, do not hold out for a little more profit; you can quickly lose much of what you have gained. The stock signals are given by a reaction that breaks the trend line and a reaction that more often than not continues swiftly to produce a price reversal. It is advantageous to anticipate this reversal signal by tracking the cyclic price position and close out before the signal is given at a better price than can be attained after the signal is given. Do not try to follow this practice on opening a position, but wait for a definite signal. If you miss a good opening execution, there is always another stock, but on closing you have to live with your existing position.

The daily high-low-close plot of the four stocks in Figure 10–5, for

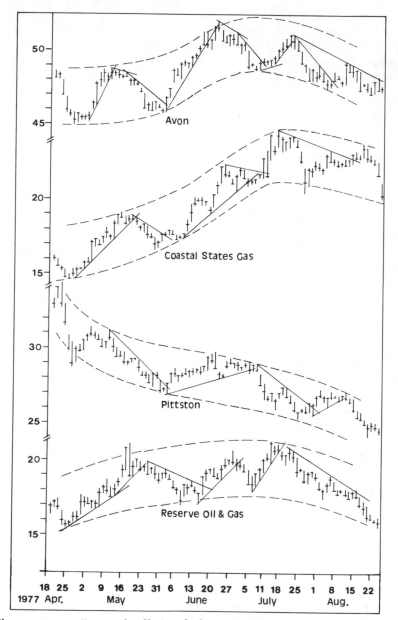

Figure 10–5. Buy and sell signals for individual stocks are produced when the price breaks the trend line.

the same time period, illustrates a wide variation in performance. Coastal States Gas is in a strong intermediate uptrend that started in the fall of 1976 at a price of about 9. In contrast, Pittston is in an intermediate downtrend that started in mid-1976 at a high of about 47. Avon is in a mild uptrend that has not made much progress for the past year, and Reserve Oil and Gas shows a top area after a sharp rise during 1976. The trading cycle movements are brought out by the envelope boundries shown as dashed lines. Trend lines are drawn to illustrate how they may be used to determine buy and sell points. Whether you enter into a buy or sell transaction at these points should be based on additional analysis of the stock and market movements to determine if the price is expected to move far enough to make a sufficient profit after commissions to compensate for the risks involved.

Not all trend lines that can be drawn are shown in Figure 10–5. It is important to note how prices consistently move to the trend line, even for short movements. Trading cycle movements against the intermediate trend do not, in general, produce enough price change to be worth following. For example, you would buy Coastal States Gas calls but would buy puts of Pittston.

11 Option Volatility

A favorite pastime of option analysts is "premium watching." Are option premiums high or low? Is it a good time to write options? You can get reports on how many options gained and decreased in price during the week. Whether the premiums increased or decreased in price depends largely on whether stocks increased or decreased, and this does not tell you much about the options market. Reports on the level of premiums relative to normal values of the options are more informative as to what options are doing. The changing factor, in which you are interested, is the time value. It takes a little calculation to obtain this value, and, further, it must be analyzed in terms of the individual stock and its price and the time to expiration. This involves considerable work.

VOLATILITY MEASURES OPTION SENTIMENT

Our option volatility value V has been defined to include option market sentiment as well as individual stock appraisal. It removes the intrinsic value from the option price, eliminates the effect of stock price, and provides an appraisal of the option market and the individual stock. It is thus a very meaningful number for comparing option market conditions. Moving averages of option volatility values for stocks or groups of stocks can be maintained for comparative purposes. Although the general stock market situation influences the option volatilities, there is in addition the independent option market influence. This measure is not difficult to produce and is worthy of attention.

OPTION TRENDS

The options volatility factor V adjusts the option equations to the characteristics of the individual stock and to the overall market sentiment. These quantities do not change rapidly in the absence of unusual circumstances but may vary considerably over a long period of time. The value of V is a measure of the level of option premiums. Conservative stocks normally have low values of V, and the more volatile stocks support higher premiums. The changes in market and stock characteristics vary over extended periods of time, resulting in the V values exhibiting long-term trends.

Figure 11–1 illustrates how the V values have changed over a 4-year period for several stocks with widely different characteristics. The value of V was determined at monthly intervals, using the closing price

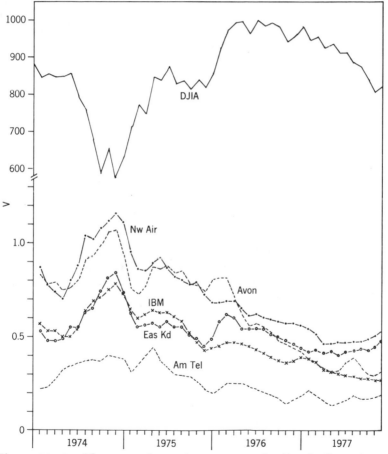

Figure 11–1.   Three-month moving average of call volatilities for five stocks and the closing price of the DJIA.

as of the first Friday of each month for the striking prices nearest above and below the stock price, when available, and the average found. A centered 3-month moving average for calls is plotted in the figure. For comparison, the closing price of the DJIA is plotted as a solid line. The trends are of interest, but more time must elapse before specific conclusions can be reached. Such curves may be used to judge the level of premiums at any given time relative to past experience.

PUTS AND CALLS COMPARED

The options volatility for puts and calls must be separately determined. The volatilities for the puts and calls for those stocks for which puts were traded were determined for the first 10 days of the start-up in trading puts. The values for the available options were averaged for each day, then the average for the 10 days found, together with the standard deviation. The results are tabulated in Table 11–1. The put pricing was as stable as for calls during this start-up period.

Table 11–2 provides similar information to that of Table 11–1 for the 10-week period after the start of put trading, using weekly closing prices. The data confirm the conclusions drawn from Table 11–1. As greater time spans are averaged, the option volatility values are expected to show greater variations that would result in larger standard deviations.

It is seen that the volatilities for a put generally differ from the corresponding call, sometimes greater but usually less, during the time period examined. The higher values of volatilities are associated with stocks expected to make the larger price move, and the lower values associated with the more conservative stocks. One might expect the difference between put and call volatilities to have directional implications; that is, if the put volatility is larger than the corresponding call volatility, the assessment is that the underlying stock is expected to move downward in the near term. As a normal relationship, one might expect a bias toward one direction, depending on which type of option is the more appealing to the market. You may be interested in studying these relationships over more extended periods of time and in different types of markets.

Of the twenty-four stocks on which both puts and calls were traded in the 10-week period after the start of put trading, six showed no significant difference between put and call volatilities, and in two the put volatilities were significantly higher. During this period, the bias was toward higher premiums for calls than for corresponding puts.

Table 11–1

Average option volatility and standard deviation for the first 10 days of trading after the start of put trading on June 3, 1977, for those stocks on which puts were traded on the five exchanges.

Stock	Average Volatility		Standard Deviation	
	Call	Put	Call	Put
CBOE				
Avon	.32	.33	.01	.01
EasKd	.42	.37	.03	.01
GM	.27	.30	.01	.02
IBM	.28	.22	.01	.01
Honwll	.39	.32	.01	.01
AMEX				
Aetna	.37	.28	.03	.02
Mesa Pt	.52	.36	.03	.03
Westng	.49	.35	.03	.03
ASA	.62	.47	.02	.03
Res OG	.71	.53	.03	.02
Philadelphia				
Allis C	.47	.42	.03	.03
Cont O	.39	.36	.03	.03
A Hess	.45	.34	.03	.02
Inexco	.71	.55	.07	.02
Pttstn	.40	.43	.03	.02
Pacific				
Levi	.47	.38	.03	.03
ABC	.42	.31	.02	.02
Heubln	.41	.44	.03	.03
Scher	.36	.38	.05	.03
San Fe	.50	.36	.03	.02
Midwest				
Crrier	.47	.42	.02	.05
Corn Gl	.34	.41	.03	.05
Nw Ind	.30	.39	.02	.02
Revlon	.35	.44	.03	.01

VOLATILITY VARIATIONS

There are times when in-the-money options of a stock or of a group of stocks will be valued higher or lower than the out-of-the money op-

Table 11–2

Average option volatility and standard deviation of the weekly closing
values for the first 10 weeks of trading after the start of put trading on June
3, 1977, for those stocks on which puts were traded on the five exchanges.

| | Average Volatility | | Standard Deviation | |
Stock	Call	Put	Call	Put
CBOE				
Avon	.33	.32	.03	.02
EasKd	.42	.35	.03	.02
GM	.24	.30	.02	.02
IBM	.27	.23	.02	.02
Honwll	.41	.33	.04	.01
AMEX				
Aetna	.36	.32	.03	.03
Mesa Pt	.56	.41	.05	.07
Westng	.49	.35	.03	.02
ASA	.63	.46	.06	.07
Res OG	.74	.52	.05	.03
Philadelphia				
Allis C	.49	.37	.02	.04
Cont O	.36	.35	.03	.02
A Hess	.50	.36	.06	.02
Inexco	.73	.57	.07	.03
Pttstn	.44	.43	.05	.03
Pacific				
Levi	.47	.38	.07	.04
ABC	.41	.34	.02	.02
Heubln	.46	.42	.04	.03
Scher	.39	.38	.05	.04
San Fe	.52	.37	.04	.01
Midwest				
Crrier	.51	.43	.06	.04
Corn Gl	.33	.37	.03	.04
Nw Ind	.37	.35	.05	.04
Revlon	.40	.41	.03	.02

tions. This deviation from normal shows up in the option volatility
values. There are also times when premiums are higher or lower than
normal as a function of time to expiration, which is likewise reflected in
the option volatility values. In analyzing the general options market,

you may want to examine these variations. When the deviations are significant, it may affect your choice of strategy.

Figure 11–2 plots a 3-week moving average of the in-the-money and the out-of-the-money call option volatility V average for six stocks over a period of 20 months. The stocks selected for this average have an active options market, wide range of stock prices, and wide range of option volatilities. The stocks used were Avon, Eastman Kodak, General Motors, IBM, Mesa Petroleum, and Westinghouse. The call option volatility was found for the striking price nearest above the stock price for out-of-the-money calls for each of the three times to expiration, using Friday's closing quotations when available. Expiration times less than 30 days and quoted call values of 1/16 point were eliminated, because the low time values may not give a reliable value for V. An average volatility for the group of six stocks was found each week, using the weekly values for that week, or the last weekly value if no striking price was available for out-of-the-money calls. A 3-week moving average was taken and plotted (dotted line) in Figure 11–2 on a centered time axis. In a similar manner, an in-the-money moving average was found and plotted as the solid line.

Figure 11–2 indicates that the average of the in-the-money and out-of-the-money option volatilities for calls does not differ greatly and tends to move together in the same direction but usually is slightly different, with the value for in-the-money calls being sometimes greater and sometimes less than the value for out-of-the-money calls. The differences are greater on an individual stock basis than on the average.

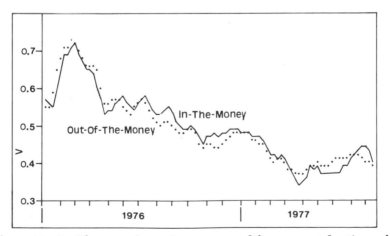

Figure 11– 2. Three-week moving average of the average of option volatilities for six stocks for in-the-money and out-of-the money calls.

and at times the situation for one stock may be reversed to that for some other stock. When looking for overvalued or undervalued options, an analysis of the option volatilities for the individual stocks is very useful. When analyzing the options market as a whole, an average such as in Figure 11–2 allows comparisons with the past. A single average, combining the in-the-money and out-of-the-money volatilties, may be used for this purpose if preferred. Similar results are found for put options.

EFFECT OF EX-DIVIDEND DATE

When a stock goes ex-dividend, its value is less by the amount of the dividend. Exchange-traded option striking prices are not adjusted for dividends; therefore, the option premium will change suddenly to adjust to the new value of the stock when the stock goes ex-dividend. For small dividends this may not be apparent, but if the dividend is large, there may be a considerable difference in option premiums between the day before and the day of ex-dividend. In fact, the premium value anticipates this change, and call premiums will run low and put premiums will run high for sometime prior to the ex-dividend date. As an illustration, IBM dividend of $2.50 was paid to stock of record of August 10, 1977, going ex-dividend 4 business days prior, August 4, 1977. The time values for the nearest in-the-money options are as follows:

Date	Stock Price	Striking Price	Option Time Values		
			October	January	April
8-3-77	269¾	260 call	2⅝	5⅞	9⅝
		280 put	4⅞	7¼	9⅛
8-4-77	268⅝	260 call	4½	8¼	11⅞
		280 put	1⅝	4⅛	6⅞

Note that if the $2.50 dividend is added to the time values of the call for the day prior to the stock going ex-dividend, the result approximates the corresponding time value of the call on the following day. Similarly, if the dividend is subtracted from the put time values, the result corresponds to the put values on the following day. This effect is one of anticipation of a change in intrinsic value, but it is reflected as a change of time value, as we calculate time values. These changes may begin to appear several weeks before the ex-dividend date, and they will distort

Table 11–3

Quoted price of out-of-the-money options for IBM at the time the stock goes ex-dividend $2.50 compared with normal values had no dividend been anticipated.

			Option Values			
Date	Stock Price	Striking Price	October	January	April	
8-3-77	269¾	280 call	3	6⅝	9½	Quoted
			4.03	7.64	10.62	Normal
		260 put	4⅜	7¼	9½	Quoted
			3.65	6.95	9.70	Normal
8-4-77	268⅝	280 call	3½	7½	10⅜	Quoted
			3.68	7.20	10.14	Normal
		260 put	3⅜	6¾	8¾	Quoted
			3.87	7.25	10.02	Normal
	267¼	280 call	3.33	6.74	9.61	Normal
		260 put	4.23	7.67	10.47	Normal

the calculation of option volatility as well as affecting the option premiums. For low dollar value, as distinguished from percentage value, of dividends, you need not be concerned, but if the stock pays a high dividend, perhaps as a special, you should take the dividend and its ex-dividend date into account.

For out-of-the-money options, the ex-dividend effect is less, since there is no intrinsic value. The effect is one of anticipation of a stock price drop by the amount of the dividend on ex-dividend date. The change in option value is due to the stock price factor in the option equations. This results in the call options being underpriced, relative to past prices, and puts being overpriced. IBM did not drop the full amount of approximately 2½ points but only 1⅛ of a point. Table 11–3 gives closing quoted option values for the quoted stock price for August 3 and 4 and the normal values, using a 5-day moving average for the option volatilities. In addition, normal values are given for a price of 267¼ as of August 4, corresponding to the price IBM would have closed at if it had been down by the dividend. These values compare favorably with the quoted values on August 3.

OPTION PRICES LAG STOCK PRICES

When the price of a stock makes a significant move in either direction, there is a tendency for the price of the option to lag slightly in time. This is found to be the case for both puts and calls and for both the in- and out-of-the-money options. This is not to say that option prices fail to move but only that they do not move far enough immediately when the stock price changes. We have used the option volatility to measure option values independent of the intrinsic value and level of stock price. In general, when the stock price increases, the call volatility will decrease because the quoted call price is lower than it should be, and the put volatility will increase because the quoted put value does not decrease as much as it should. Conversely, for a stock price decrease, the call volatility will be larger because the quoted call value remains too large, and the put volatility will decrease; that is, the put and call volatilities will move in opposite directions from their average

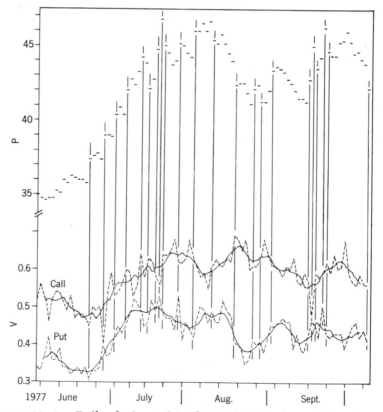

Figure 11–3.   Daily closing price of Mesa Petroleum and the put and call volatilities (dotted lines) with their 5-day moving average (solid line). Vertical lines designate days on which stock price moved by 1 point or more.

values. This effect is illustrated in Figure 11–3. The daily closing price of Mesa Petroleum is plotted with the average put and call option volatilities, using the options whose striking price is nearest above and below the stock price and for the three times to expiration. These are shown as dotted lines. A 5-day moving average is found for the volatilities, which may be considered a normal reference value, and is plotted as a solid line. Vertical lines designate days on which the closing price of the stock changed by 1 point or more from the previous closing price. Note that there is frequently a sharp 1-day deviation of the value of V from the normal value at these days and that a return to normal value usually occurs by the next day's closing.

12 Review of
Option Trading

Trading in options is like betting. To win, you seek out situations in which possible gains exceed your risks. When you place your money, you must face the possibility of losing it all if you are wrong. Do not allocate more of your funds to option trading than you can afford to lose. You play a leverage game, taking a small risk on the chance of winning a lot. Trading in options is a fast game. You may pick a stock that will rise or fall, but this is not enough. Will it move soon enough? Both selection and timing are very important. Nail down your profits early; do not let them run past your objective. They can be entirely dissipated on a minor price reversal, and time generally works against you. Waiting for a comeback can spell total loss.

LEARN TO PREDICT STOCK PRICE MOVEMENTS

Option price movement is largely dependent on the price movement of the underlying stock. You must master the art of selecting stocks whose price movement is highly predictable over the short term, that is, over a period of time corresponding to the time you want to hold a position in its options. You can find some stocks that, for a period of time, have well-behaved cyclic movements. Search these out; do not waste time on stocks whose price movement you do not understand, even though they may be recommended by others. Remember you can be a winner if you are right more often than wrong; so do not be discouraged if some do not work out. If you expect to have some losers, you will be more likely to cut your losses short. You gain both because your losses are smaller in value than your gains and because they are fewer in number.

134

Your stock price predictions must, as a minimum, give both direction and amount of move to the degree that the move will produce an acceptable profit after commissions. In some strategies you need to predict a rather exact amount of movement, not too much as well as not too little, and in some the price has to be very near a given value at a particular future time. If you cannot make such an exact prediction, select an option strategy that only requires that which you can predict with reasonable certainty.

The stocks you analyze must have options available of the type you are interested in. Watch the list of most active, those making new highs, if bullish, and those making new lows, if bearish, for good choices. You also should have a chart book giving weekly high-low-close prices for examining past history and the longer cycles and for picking out good stocks for further analysis. A daily chart on a few selected stocks should be used, preferably kept up to date by yourself, for trading cycle analysis and pinpointing buy and sell signals.

Keep a chart of the daily price movement of some market average, and keep track of its long- and short-term cyclic movements. When the market has well-defined movements, select option strategies that go with the market. When the market goes through long periods of consolidations, operate on the side of the trading cycles that are going with a longer stock price cycle.

UNDERSTAND MARKET PSYCHOLOGY

Investors and traders in stocks have made a strong distinction between operating on the long side of the market by buying stock versus the trader who will also sell short. The holding times are usually quite different, the risk differs, and short selling becomes more involved. There is some tendency to carry over these feelings to the option market and perhaps in the wrong way. In the option market, buying either puts or calls, which must be paid for in cash, represents the long side. Selling puts or calls, which you do not have and do not even have to borrow, represents the short side. The purchase of a put when you think the stock is going down in price should be thought of the same way as you consider buying a call when you expect a price rise. You should expect stock prices to go down as much as up. You may question this when looking at the market averages over many years, but if you account for inflation, it is more realistic and particularly over the last decade. There is nothing wrong with placing your dollars on what you believe; there are always those willing to place their dollars on a belief that is opposite yours. The two groups are kept in balance by the price one has to pay; this is what makes an auction market.

In the options market there are two kinds of options, and they can both be bought long or sold short. You may have your reasons against selling short; it is generally more complicated and frequently involves margin, but do not let your bias keep you out of a falling market. A falling market is as reasonable as a rising one, even though most people, including stock brokers and market advisors, would rather see a bullish market and tend to let their wishes become beliefs that get passed to you as predictions. Keep cool, stay with the basic facts, and do not be swayed by what others are saying.

BUYING OPTIONS FOR LEVERAGE

The most direct way to participate in the option market is to purchase options for capital gains. Buy calls when the stock price is expected to increase, and buy puts when it is expected to fall. This strategy provides the greatest leverage, and your risk is limited specifically to the cost of the options plus commissions. There is no margin requirement. Your profits are very directly associated with how much the underlying stock moves. Predicting the time of the move is not so critical as in many other strategies, but it must be within the life of the option, and the earlier the better, for option value will be lost by the steady erosion of the time value as time passes. Profits must be taken promptly when the price objective has been reached. Even though the stock price indicates further movement in the desired direction, it may be profitable to sell the option when in the money and open a new position out of the money, that is, roll over your position.

The stock price movement of first importance is that of the short-term trading cycle. These movements are most pronounced around the flat parts of the longer cycles, and in these situations both sides of the cycle can be used, alternating the purchase of calls and puts. When the longer cycles form a strong upward or downward trend, it is safer to trade only on that side of the trading cycle going with the trend.

Buying options a few points out of the money, which are expected to move to in the money, offers the best percentage gains.

WRITING OPTIONS

One can operate on the short side of the options market rather than on the long side, as described in the section above; that is, sell a call if the stock is expected to decrease in price, or sell a put if the stock price is expected to increase. This approach has the advantage of the time value of the options working with you instead of against you, but this advantage may be overcome by the disadvantages. If writing uncovered, you have to supply margin. Further, you stand the risk of an exercise if the stock price goes against you, causing a loss that is unlimited and subjecting you to additional commissions.

If holding stock on which covered calls are written or writing puts when short the stock, the risk is determinable for an exercise. The premiums received may produce a profit after commissions, but you gave up the chances of participating in the price movement of your stock position. If the stock price is not such as to bring forth an exercise, you pocket the premium as added income. This has its shortcomings also. Your paper losses on the stock position can be much greater than the premiums collected; so you have this risk to think about.

The strategy of writing options for profit is complex and may subject you to risks you do not want to take. If it is your policy to hold a long position in stocks no matter what, writing calls on these stocks can be a source of added income. If you choose such a program, it may be advantageous to cover your calls if they fall to a low value, since most of the profit can be had for the taking, rather than take a chance on a price reversal.

SPREADS REDUCE RISK BUT LIMIT GAINS

Spreads reduce opening costs and limit risks but also reduce possible gains. Some require a specific stock price at expiration to achieve desired profits. This is difficult to accomplish. You may want to operate not too far from expiration in order to improve your prediction of the stock price movement. Commissions increase because of involvement of two or more different options. The short option brings up the possibility of early exercise. Margin requirements must be considered, and some strategies require additional margin. The risk reduction may be small; be sure it is worth the price you pay in limiting possible gains and the added complexity.

TIMING CRITICAL FOR HORIZONTAL SPREADS

Horizontal spread values vary with stock price and option volatility. Do not open a spread unless it is normal or better. Use the option tables or formulas to check. Find the normal value of the long option when it has 90 days to expiration. This value should be at least twice the cost of opening the spread before commissions. Try to get at least ½ point on the short sale. Use calls if bullish and puts if bearish. You desire to close near expiration time of the short option, with the stock selling near the striking price. If the price moves too fast, close your position shortly after the stock moves through the striking price.

Acceptable horizontal spreads are difficult to find. Besides the requirement to find a good opening position, you must also find a stock whose price is projected to be near the striking price at the time the near-term option expires, and there is very little leeway for error.

BALANCED VERTICAL SPREADS EASY TO ANALYZE

Balanced vertical spreads are limited in value to the difference between striking prices. The stocks may move fast; there is no penalty for a price overshoot. Your opening debit should be no more than 1½ points per 5 points separation of striking prices for an acceptable risk-reward ratio. When bullish, use calls with the buy near the lower striking price for an expected rise to at least the upper striking price. When bearish, use puts with the buy near the upper striking price, expecting the price to fall to at least the lower striking price. If the spread value reaches essentially the difference between striking prices, close your position; you have all you are going to get, and your money can be better used in a new position.

Good opening situations are easy to recognize, price-time relations are not critical, proper closing positions are well defined, and the spread is not sensitive to stock price or option volatility.

UNLIMITED RISK IN RATIO SPREADS

Ratio spreads reduce initial cost and risk in one direction but introduce unlimited risk for the desired direction of price movement if it is too much.

The bullish vertical ratio spread reduces opening costs, but the conditions for success are critical. The stock price must be close to the upper striking price of the options sold at expiration time. Not only does this require good prediction, but the number of stocks that fulfill this requirement will be very limited. Having made a selection, the stock must not move too fast, or you will be forced to close to prevent unlimited loss. This high-risk possibility, when the stock moves in the direction expected but too far, overshadows the low risk against the price moving opposite to that predicted.

The vertical ratio spread can be used in a bearish strategy. The opportunities are limited by the need for several striking prices so as to be able to open at a stock price outside the spread pair on the side of the option sold short. This permits an opening credit, and only a moderate price movement can produce a gain. The price-time relation is not critical. You do have margin on the naked options and risk of exercise from the opening. You can make better profits using the bearish balanced spread.

BUTTERFLIES ARE SCARCE

The two-for-one vertical spread, just reviewed, can eliminate all risk in one direction, but protection is limited in the other price direction. For a small cost, risk can be eliminated in both directions by purchase of another option at a third striking price, which creates the butterfly spread. Limiting risk in both directions costs more than the opening debit. To make a profit, the option must approach expiration within a rather limited range of stock prices; thus timing becomes critical. Either puts or calls may be used. A major practical problem is that of finding the right conditions to open a position. Besides the usual requirement of the indicated price movement being in the proper direction and proper amount, one has to have the stock price located within rather narrow limits with respect to them. Margins are generally small, and small profits can be made with nominal pricing situations, but look for deviations that reduce the opening cost.

STRADDLES, PLAY IT BOTH WAYS

Puts and calls can be combined to form a straddle, which may be advantageous when a stock has wide and rapid price swings. If you buy a straddle near the striking price, its value will increase for a price move in either direction. If the swings are wide enough, you can close your position at a profit and take a new position near another striking price. This strategy can create a rapid turnover of funds, resulting in large annualized profits.

An alternative to the last strategy is to close only the profitable side of the straddle and wait for a price reversal to make the other side profitable. You may pyramid your position by doubling your position in the option retained, since it will be low-priced. This latter strategy could be a loser, as the stock price may not reverse but keep going, oscillating around some new level.

PUT AND CALL COMBINATIONS

Puts and calls may be combined at different striking prices. One strategy is to sell a put and a call that are both out of the money. In this combination the stock price is between two striking prices, the lower associated with the put and the upper with the call. If the stock price remains between these two striking prices at expiration, both options expire worthless, and you pocket the sale credit. You are relying on vanishing time values to turn a profit, and for this to be large requires opening the position in the more distant to expire options, which introduces a problem of price movement prediction for the longer times into the future. It is preferable to accept a moderate credit in exchange for a shorter time to expiration. Both options require margin if sold naked.

COMBINING STOCKS WITH OPTIONS

Buying a call to protect a short stock position and buying a put to protect a long stock position are known as hedges. A trading hedge of interest is to buy a put a few points in the money and the underlying stock at the same time when you expect the stock to increase in price. If the price does not move up as expected, you can exercise the put, receiving the striking price for the stock for some gain that offsets some of the cost of the put. Your risk is defined and can be rather small. This position can be turned into an equivalent vertical spread by selling a call at a higher striking price, which reduces risk further at the expense of limiting possible gains.

A FINAL WORD

There are many ways to trade options, but, fortunately, if you just want to make money, in general, the simpler are the best. A beginner is advised to purchase options for capital gain. Of first importance is picking the right stock at the right time. Option profits are dependent on the price movement of the underlying stock; learning to predict the magnitude and timing of these movements is your key to success. Selecting the proper striking price and expiration time to match the stock price movement optimizes gains, but do not play it too close; leave some room for error.

As the strategies become more complex, price-time relations become more restrictive. This not only requires better prediction but also reduces the number of acceptable situations. Next after purchasing individual options is the balanced vertical spread; opening situations are numerous and closing is not critical, but be sure the reduced risk is worth the limitation in profits.

When only purchases are involved, the maximum risk is known and is specifically the opening cost. The risk is also the opening cost for bullish balanced spreads, and it can be determined for the bearish balanced spreads. If more options are sold than purchased, the risk becomes unlimited, though it can be limited or eliminated for one direction of price movement. Risk-reducing strategies also reduce and limit possible gains; watch that the penalty on gains does not outweigh the value of the reduced risk.

Analyze the market and stock movements, and be convinced of success before opening an option position. You do not have to be in the market all the time; wait for good opportunities. Do not overtrade; limit your funds and number of positions to what you can analyze and supervise. Do not place all your eggs in a single basket; hold back funds if your selections are limited, and commit all your option funds only when you can diversify in several positions. Take losses quickly when the price does not act as expected; be willing to admit you made a mistake.

Plan your strategy; decide what risk you are willing to take; define your objectives; and choose carefully.

APPENDIXES

A Calculator Programs

If you are active in the options market, a programmable calculator is very useful. This appendix describes programs written for the Texas Instrument's Slide-rule Calculator, SR-52, but there are a number of calculators that you could select; the mathematics is not complicated and should present no problem. It is important to understand your particular calculator, and for those not familiar with the SR-52 some features will be reviewed so that you can understand the programs and adapt them to your particular machine.

The SR-52 has *user-defined keys*, A to E, and *A' to *E' reached through the second function key, making ten in all; the asterisk denotes the second function operation. A program segment may be established to be executed by any one of these keys. For example, when entering data into a memory register, the data are merely keyed in, showing on the display; then the proper user-defined key is pressed to place the displayed value in the designated memory. Further, if the program calls for computing some function that is dependent on this one datum only, the function may be immediately computed and the result stored for future use. These program segments will appear in the programs as, for example, *LBL A, they may be written in any order, and the data entered in any order. The final calculation can be initiated by pressing a designated key, such as E; it appears in the program as *LBL E. If user-defined keys are not available on your machine, the data can be entered into the memories by a store function, and the program may be started by a run key.

Any one of the ten keys may be used in the body of the program to designate a program location to go to under certain conditions. Also, most keys, when preceded by *LBL, can be used to designate program locations that can be used in the program in branching operations or subroutines. A subroutine is designated by SBR. As an example, the second function of the numerical key 3 could designate a subroutine thus, SBR *3'. A subroutine must be terminated by the *rtn, which returns the program to the next step of the main program after calling the subroutine.

The SR-52 can compare two numbers, asking whether their difference is positive or whether it is zero. The inverse key (INV), when pressed ahead of the questions above, determines whether the difference is negative or whether it is not zero. These are used for branching operations; if the answer is yes, the program goes to the designated location but, if no, continues on the main program.

There are five flags that may be set if the program goes through a particular branch. Later in the program a branching operation may be encountered where the direction taken depends on whether the flag is set or not.

In the SR-52 memories are designated by two-digit numbers, memory two being 02. The program locations are designated by three digits starting with 000.

The individual programs will be described and particular features pointed out to facilitate understanding them. This will be followed by a program listing in which each program step is designated by the key function and numbered by the three-digit program location number. The program segments will be separated in the listings for ease in understanding. Each segment is headed by the *LBL designation, followed by a key operation that identifies the segment. In discussing the program, we will omit the *LBL and refer to the program segment by its identifying key operation. The SR-52 and some other calculators can store programs on a magnetic card for future use, which saves time and prevents errors once your program has been checked.

PROGRAM I

Normal Values of Puts and Calls:
This program allows you to compute the value of either the put or call using Equations (9–5) to (9–8) and their expanded functions given by Equations (9–2) and (9–9). The known data are entered by user-defined keys A to D at the program locations designated with the program actions as described:

A. Location 049-056. Stock price P is stored in memory 01, and the number of decimal digits to be displayed fixed at two (*fix 2).

B. Location 057-062. Striking price S is stored in memory 02.

C. Location 063-092. Days to expiration D is stored in memory 03, and the function A of Equation (9–2) is computed and stored in memory 11.

D. Location 093-098. Option volatility V is stored in memory 04.

These data may be entered in any order, and one value varied as you may desire to see what effect it has on the option value without reentering the other values.

At program location 070 a dummy STO program step is used that has the effect of holding the displayed value of step 068 (square root of D) to be used as the entry for taking the logarithm. If your computer does not have this type of operation, you could recall D from memory 03 and take the square root.

The time value as given by Equation (9–9) is computed by program steps 000 to 048 and is programmed as a subroutine *6'. This program segment is the most used part and so is placed at the beginning to reduce the search time when called for. It first computes PAV and stores in memory 12 (steps 000 to 016) and then finds (P-S) and stores in 13 (017 to 027). The absolute value of (P-S) is taken (028 and 029), divided by 2 and by PAV, sign is changed, exponent is evaluated, multiplied by PAV, and the result is stored in memory 08, this being the time value of Equation (9–9). The program is returned to the program segment that called up the subroutine.

Computation of the option value is initiated by user-defined key E or *E'. Key E (step 099) produces the call value, and key *E' (step 115) produces the put value. Each key first calls for subroutine *6', which computes the time value and then recalls the stored value (P-S) from memory 13. At this point, a decision is made as to whether the option is in the money or out of the money by determining whether (P-S) is positive or negative. If a put is being computed (user key *E'), the question if positive is asked, and if the answer is yes, the stock price P is greater than or equal to the striking price S, and the put is out of the money, and its value is merely the time value stored in memory 08. In this case, the program is directed to go to location *7' which is found at step 131, which recalls the value in memory 08 and halts the program, displaying the desired value. If the answer had not been yes, meaning negative, the program drops down to the next step, which changes the sign of (P-S) to give a positive value, which is the intrinsic value, and then adds the time value and halts, displaying the put value.

If a call is being computed, the process is similar, but the question is whether (P-S) is negative (INV *if pos) at steps 106–107. If yes, the call is out of the money, and we go to *7' and display the time value. If the answer is no, (P-S) is positive and is the intrinsic value, the program drops down, adding the time value and halts.

If your calculator is limited in program steps, the computation can be shortened. First, you could substitute the value of A found from Appendix C for the program segment C, which computes A from D. Second, you merely compute the time value as in program segment *6', which gives the out-of-the-money option value. For in-the-money options you merely add the intrinsic value.

PROGRAM I Listing

000	*LBL		*LBL		*LBL		*LBL	115	*LBL
	*6'	050	A		C		D		*E'
	RCL		*fix	065	STO	095	STO		SBR
	0		2		0		0		*6'
	1		STO		3		4		RCL
005	x		0		*√x		HLT	120	1
	RCL	055	1		+				3
	1		HLT	070	STO				*if pos
	1				ln				*7'
	x				+				+/−
010	RCL				RCL			125	+
	0				0				RCL
	½		*LBL	075	3				0
	=	B			x		*LBL		8
	STO		STO		.				=
015	1	060	0		0	100	E	130	HLT
	2		2		1		SBR		
	RCL		HLT	080	3		*6'		
	0				−		RCL		
	1				1		1		*LBL
020	−				=	105	3		*7'
	RCL				÷		INV		RCL
	0			085	1		*if pos		0
	2				0		*7'	135	8
	=				0		+		HLT
025	STO				=	110	RCL		
	1				STO		0		
	3			090	1		8		
	*x²				1		=		
	*√x				HLT		HLT		
030	÷								
	2								
	÷								
	RCL								
	1								
035	2								
	=								
	+/−								
	INV								
	ln								
040	x								
	RCL								
	1								
	2								
	=								
045	STO								
	0								
	8								
	*rtn								

Program I
Instructions

Enter data (in any order)	Press—
Stock price P	A
Striking price S	B
Calendar days to expiration D	C
Option volatility V	D

Compute

Call value	E
Put value	*E'

TEST (change program step 052 from 2 to 9 for full display)

Enter data—	Then Press—	Answer
P = 45	E	7.114814159
S = 40	*E'	2.114814159
D = 100		
V = 0.7		
P = 40	E	1.737530509
S = 45	*E'	6.737530509
D = 100		
V = 0.7		

MEMORIES	Used for—
01	P
02	S
03	D
04	V
08	T
11	A
12	PAV
13	P–S

PROGRAM II

Computing Volatility:

You may determine option volatility by the methods described in Chapter 2, including using the tables in Appendix D, or you may use Program I by substituting estimates of V and solving for the option value until it is in substantial agreement with the quoted option value.

Program II carries out the substitution, makes the comparisons, and increments the value of V until it is within 0.01 of the exact value for the quoted prices and stated conditions. Much of the program is about the same as in Program I, such as segment *6', which is the subroutine that computes the time value, and the segments that take the input data, A, B, C, and D. The quoted option value is entered on segment E. The value of V is estimated as a start, and if doing a series of computations in which V should be the same, the last computed value is left as being as good a guess as any. The computation is started by pressing *A' for the call volatility and *B' for the put volatility.

The program procedure for both the put and call volatility is first to find (P-S) by the subroutine *9', determine its sign, and if the option is out of the money, the quoted option value is recalled and stored in memory 08 as the time value. If the option was in the money, the program goes to subroutine *7', where (P-S) is subtracted from the quoted option value to obtain the time value for storage in the time value memory 08. Subroutines *7' and *8' are terminated by the *rset function, which in the SR-52 resets the flags and resets the program counter to position 000, which causes the program to proceed with the computation. First, the time value is computed for the data input values, using an assumed value of V, by subroutine *6', and then the quoted time value is subtracted, and a comparison is made by asking if the difference is positive. If yes, the program goes to segment *1', which sets flag 2 and asks if flag 1 has been set. If flag 1 has not been set, the value of V is decreased by 0.03 and the program reset to segment *0', by the GTO instruction, to compute a new time value. If flag 1 had been set, it would mean that a previous comparison of time values gave a negative result and the program would then have continued, resulting in increasing the value of V and returning to the beginning for another try. When encountering the situation in which the flag in the other channel has been set, it is then known that the sign of the difference in the computed and quoted time values has been reversed; so the program is directed to segment *2' or *3', where the value of V is incremented by only 0.01, and this continues until the sign of the difference is again reversed, as is determined by flags 3 and 4, in which case the program

PROGRAM II Listing

000	*LBL		*LBL		*LBL	110	*LBL		*LBL		*LBL
	*0'	025	*6'		*1'		A	155	*A'		*9'
	SBR		RCL	065	*st flg		*fix		SBR		RCL
	*6'		0		2		2		*9'	195	0
	−		1		*if flg		STO		INV		1
005	RCL		×		1	115	0		*if pos		−
	0	030	RCL		*3'		1	160	*8'		RCL
	8		1	070	.		HLT		+/−		0
	=		1		0				GTO	200	2
	*if pos		×		3				*7'		=
010	*1'		RCL		INV		*LBL				STO
	*st flg	035	0		SUM		B				1
	1		4	075	0	120	STO		*LBL	205	3
	*if flg		=		4		0	165	*B'		*rtn
	2		STO		GTO		2		SBR		
015	*2'		1		*0'		HLT		*9'		
	.	040	2						*if pos		*LBL
	0		*1/x						*8'		*4'
	3		×		*LBL		*LBL	170	GTO		RCL
	SUM		RCL	080	*2'	125	C		*7'		0
020	0		1		*st flg		STO			210	4
	4	045	3		3		0				HLT
	GTO		÷		.		3		*LBL		
	*0'		2		0		* √x		*7'		
			=	085	1	130	+		+		*LBL
			*x²		SUM		STO	175	RCL		D
		050	* √x		0		ln		0		STO
			+/−		4		+		5	215	0
			INV		*if flg		RCL		=		4
			ln	090	4	135	0		STO		HLT
			×		*4'		3	180	0		
		055	RCL		GTO		×		8		
			1		*0'		.		*rset		*LBL
			2				0				E
			−			140	1			220	STO
			STO		*LBL		3		*LBL		0
		060	0	095	*3'		−		*8'		5
			9		*st flg		1	185	RCL		HLT
			*rtn		4		=		0		
					.	145	÷		5		
					0		1		STO		
				100	1		0		0		
					INV		0	190	8		
					SUM		=		*rset		
					0	150	STO				
					4		1				
				105	*if flg		1				
					3		HLT				
					*4'						
					GTO						
					*0'						

goes to segment *4', which recalls the stored value of V, displaying it, and the program halts.

This program could be shortened by having only one size of increment for V. The size of the increments may be changed as desired, the larger value shortening the computational time for bad guesses for V and the smaller value determining the final accuracy of the computation. For the values of 0.03 and 0.01, the running time varies from about 15 seconds upward, depending on how many iterations are required.

Program II

Instructions

Enter data (in any order)	Press—
Stock price P	A
Striking price S	B
Calendar days to expiration D	C
Option volatility estimate V	D
Quoted option price O	E

Compute

Call volatility	*A'
Put volatility	*B'

TEST

Enter data—

			Press—	Answer
P = 45	and	O = 7	*A'	0.67
S = 40		O = 2	*B'	0.67
D = 100				
*V = 0.7				

* Note that a solution will be obtained for any starting value of V, but the answer can differ by 0.01, depending on the direction of convergence.

MEMORIES   Used for—

01	P
02	S
03	D
04	V
05	O
08	Quoted time value
09	Computed time value
11	A
12	PAV
13	P–S

PROGRAM III

Moving Average:

This program is useful for finding the moving average of a span of ten items when you are computing a long series. You need only to key in the new number to get the average of the last ten items. The span length can be varied, as is obvious by inspection of the program listing, by changing the number of program steps of the form *EXC mm SUM 00 and the division at the end. The operation *EXC exchanges the displayed value with the value stored in the memory designated following the *EXC operation. The program procedure is to move the previous input numbers down through the memory chain and discard the oldest value that is brought up to the display on the last *EXC operation (memory 11 in this program). As each value is displayed, it is accumulated in memory 00, to be recalled at the end of the program, divided by the number of items in the span, and the result displayed. When starting, the displayed values should be disregarded until ten values have been entered. The program operation is simply to enter the data through user-defined key A, one item at a time.

If you are maintaining a moving average on a continuing basis, you will probably find it easier to compute it as described in Chapter 10 in the section on moving averages.

PROGRAM III Listing

000	*LBL	015	0	030	1	045	0	060	0
	A		0		5		0		0
	STO		*EXC		SUM		*EXC		÷
	0		1		0		1		1
	0		7		0		2		0
005	*EXC	020	SUM	035	*EXC	050	SUM	065	=
	1		0		1		0		HLT
	9		0		4		0		
	SUM		*EXC		SUM		*EXC		
	0		1		0		1		
010	0	025	6	040	0	055	1		
	*EXC		SUM		*EXC		SUM		
	1		0		1		0		
	8		0		3		0		
	SUM		*EXC		SUM		RCL		

PROGRAM IV

Modified Moving Average:

The modified moving average (see Chapter 10, under "Breadth") subtracts the average value rather than the oldest item, which reduces the drop-off error of the true moving average. The modified average is useful when we are only interested in the changes, rather than the values themselves, and has been recommended for the overbought-oversold indicator and the upside-downside-volume curves.

The new data item is entered through user-defined key A, and the result is displayed as in Program III. One important difference is that the old average value must be stored in memory register 01 at the start. The *fix 0 (program location 018) causes rounding to whole numbers for the display. The span is for ten items.

PROGRAM IV Listing

000	*LBL	010	+
	A		RCL
	−		0
	RCL		1
	0		=
005	1	015	STO
	=		0
	÷		1
	1		*fix
	0		0
		020	HLT

PROGRAM V

Complete Options Program:

It is convenient to store both the option value formula and the option volatility formula on the same magnetic card. Some of the program segments are common to both programs. The combined program is very much like the individual programs, but some small changes were made to reduce the number of steps. A different method is used in carrying out the iteration for option volatility. The absolute difference between the tentative time value found in segment *6', for an assumed value of V, and the quoted value stored in memory 08 is found in the first thirteen program steps. Its sign is changed and added to 0.03. If the sum is positive, it means the assumed value of V was good enough so that the computed time value differed from the quoted time value by less than 1/32 point, in which case the program goes to segment *4', displays the value of V, and halts. If this test fails, the value of V in memory 04 is changed by an amount proportional to the error in time value, adjusted by dividing by PA, to approximate the correction required. The effect is to make a large change in V when the error is large and then smaller changes as the desired value of V is approached. This method has the advantage of reducing the number of iterations and thus reducing the running time for the program, particularly when the first assumption for the value of V is bad. For most practical purposes, this method is preferred to that in Program II.

Note at step 140 there is a Go To instruction and the following step, *LBL, serves as the location for the Go To instruction and for the program segment *5', saving a program step.

The data are entered as in the individual programs, and use of the memories is the same. The computations are initiated as follows:

Compute call option   Press *D'   Compute call volatility Press *A'
Compute put option   Press *E'   Compute put volatility Press *B'

PROGRAM V Listing

000 *LBL	*LBL	*LBL	100 *LBL	*LBL	*LBL
*0'	*6'	A	C	*C'	*3'
SBR	RCL	STO	STO	+	190 *st flg
*6'	0	0	0	GTO	0
–	040 1	080 1	3	150 *LBL	*rtn
005 RCL	x	HLT	105 * √x	*5'	
0	RCL		+	HLT	
8	1		STO		
=	1	*LBL	ln		*LBL
STO	045 =	B	+		*D'
010 0	STO	STO	110 RCL	*LBL	195 SBR
7	1	085 0	0	*LBL	*9'
*x²	0	2	3	155 RCL	SBR
* √x	x	HLT	x	0	*6'
+/–	050 RCL		.	5	INV
015 +	0		115 0	=	200 *if flg
.	4		1	STO	0
0	=	*LBL	3	160 0	*5'
3	STO	D	–	8	+
=	055 1	090 STO	1	*rset	RCL
020 *if pos	2	0	120 =		205 1
*4'	*1/x	4	÷		3
RCL	x	HLT	1	*LBL	=
0	RCL		0	*9'	HLT
7	060 1		0	165 RCL	
025 ÷	3	*LBL	125 =	0	
RCL	÷	095 E	STO	1	*LBL
1	2	STO	1	–	210 *E'
0	=	0	1	RCL	SBR
=	065 *x²	5	HLT	170 0	*9'
030 +/–	* √x	HLT		2	SBR
SUM	+/–		130 *LBL	=	*6'
0	INV		*A'	STO	215 *if flg
4	ln		SBR	1	0
GTO	070 x		*9'	175 3	*5'
035 *0'	RCL		INV	*if pos	–
	1		135 *if pos	*3'	RCL
	2		*LBL	INV	220 1
	=		+/–	*st flg	3
	075 *rtn		*C'	180 0	=
			*LBL	*rtn	HLT
			140 *B'	*LBL	
			SBR	*4'	
			*9'	185 RCL	
			*if pos	0	
			*LBL	4	
			145 *C'	HLT	

B Number of Days Between Dates

The number of days an option has to go to expiration may be found from the following table by subtracting the day number for the present date from that for the expiration date. If the expiration date is beyond the end of the current year, first add 365 to the day number of the expiration date.

Day Number for Each Day of the Year

Day of Mo.	Jan.	Feb.	Mar.	Apr.	May	Jun.	Jul.	Aug.	Sep.	Oct.	Nov.	Dec.	Day of Mo.
1	1	32	60	91	121	152	182	213	244	274	305	335	1
2	2	33	61	92	122	153	183	214	245	275	306	336	2
3	3	34	62	93	123	154	184	215	246	276	307	337	3
4	4	35	63	94	124	155	185	216	247	277	308	338	4
5	5	36	64	95	125	156	186	217	248	278	309	339	5
6	6	37	65	96	126	157	187	218	249	279	310	340	6
7	7	38	66	97	127	158	188	219	250	280	311	341	7
8	8	39	67	98	128	159	189	220	251	282	312	342	8
9	9	40	68	99	129	160	190	221	252	282	313	343	9
10	10	41	69	100	130	161	191	???	253	283	314	344	10
11	11	42	70	101	131	162	192	223	254	284	315	345	11
12	12	43	71	102	132	163	193	224	255	285	316	346	12
13	13	44	72	103	133	164	194	225	256	286	317	347	13
14	14	45	73	104	134	165	195	226	257	287	318	348	14
15	15	46	74	105	135	166	196	227	258	288	319	349	15
16	16	47	75	106	136	167	197	228	259	289	320	350	16
17	17	48	76	107	137	168	198	229	260	290	321	351	17
18	18	49	77	108	138	169	199	230	261	291	322	352	18
19	19	50	78	109	139	170	200	231	262	292	323	353	19
20	20	51	79	110	140	171	201	232	263	293	324	354	20
21	21	52	80	111	141	172	202	233	264	294	325	355	21
22	22	53	81	112	142	173	203	234	265	295	326	356	22
23	23	54	82	113	143	174	204	235	266	296	327	357	23
24	24	55	83	114	144	175	205	236	267	297	328	358	24
25	25	56	84	115	145	176	206	237	268	298	329	359	25
26	26	57	85	116	146	177	207	238	269	299	330	360	26
27	27	58	86	117	147	178	208	239	270	300	331	361	27
28	28	59	87	118	148	179	209	240	271	301	332	362	28
29	29	*	88	119	149	180	210	241	272	302	333	363	29
30	30		89	120	150	181	211	242	273	303	334	364	30
31	31		90		151		212	243		304		365	31

* Add 1 to the numbers after this date if a leap year.

C *A* Values

Values of *A* for *D* Days to Option Expiration
in the Function $A = (\sqrt{D} + \ln \sqrt{D} + 0.013D - 1) \div 100$

D	A	D	A	D	A	D	A	D	A	D	A
1	.000	51	.088	101	.127	151	.158	201	.184	251	.209
2	.008	52	.089	102	.127	152	.158	202	.185	252	.209
3	.013	53	.090	103	.128	153	.159	203	.185	253	.210
4	.017	54	.090	104	.129	154	.159	204	.186	254	.210
5	.021	55	.091	105	.129	155	.160	205	.186	255	.211
6	.024	56	.092	106	.130	156	.160	206	.187	256	.211
7	.027	57	.093	107	.131	157	.161	207	.187	257	.211
8	.030	58	.094	108	.131	158	.162	208	.188	258	.212
9	.032	59	.095	109	.132	159	.162	209	.188	259	.212
10	.034	60	.096	110	.133	160	.163	210	.189	260	.213
11	.037	61	.097	111	.133	161	.163	211	.189	261	.213
12	.039	62	.097	112	.134	162	.164	212	.190	262	.214
13	.041	63	.098	113	.135	163	.164	213	.190	263	.214
14	.042	64	.099	114	.135	164	.165	214	.191	264	.215
15	.044	65	.100	115	.136	165	.165	215	.191	265	.215
16	.046	66	.101	116	.137	166	.166	216	.192	266	.216
17	.048	67	.102	117	.137	167	.167	217	.192	267	.216
18	.049	68	.102	118	.138	168	.167	218	.193	268	.217
19	.051	69	.103	119	.138	169	.168	219	.193	269	.217
20	.052	70	.104	120	.139	170	.168	220	.194	270	.217
21	.054	71	.105	121	.140	171	.169	221	.194	271	.218
22	.055	72	.106	122	.140	172	.169	222	.195	272	.218
23	.057	73	.106	123	.141	173	.170	223	.195	273	.219
24	.058	74	.107	124	.142	174	.170	224	.196	274	.219
25	.059	75	.108	125	.142	175	.171	225	.196	275	.220
26	.061	76	.109	126	.143	176	.171	226	.197	276	.220
27	.062	77	.109	127	.143	177	.172	227	.197	277	.221
28	.063	78	.110	128	.144	178	.172	228	.198	278	.221
29	.064	79	.111	129	.145	179	.173	229	.198	279	.221
30	.066	80	.112	130	.145	180	.174	230	.199	280	.222
31	.067	81	.113	131	.146	181	.174	231	.199	281	.222
32	.068	82	.113	132	.146	182	.175	232	.200	282	.223
33	.069	83	.114	133	.147	183	.175	233	.200	283	.223
34	.070	84	.115	134	.148	184	.176	234	.201	284	.224
35	.071	85	.115	135	.148	185	.176	235	.201	285	.224
36	.073	86	.116	136	.149	186	.177	236	.202	286	.225
37	.074	87	.117	137	.149	187	.177	237	.202	287	.225
38	.075	88	.118	138	.150	188	.178	238	.203	288	.225
39	.076	89	.118	139	.151	189	.178	239	.203	289	.226
40	.077	90	.119	140	.151	190	.179	240	.204	290	.226
41	.078	91	.120	141	.152	191	.179	241	.204	291	.227
42	.079	92	.120	142	.152	192	.180	242	.204	292	.227
43	.080	93	.121	143	.153	193	.180	243	.205	293	.228
44	.081	94	.122	144	.154	194	.181	244	.205	294	.228
45	.082	95	.123	145	.154	195	.181	245	.206	295	.229
46	.083	96	.123	146	.155	196	.182	246	.206	296	.229
47	.084	97	.124	147	.155	197	.182	247	.207	297	.229
48	.085	98	.125	148	.156	198	.183	248	.207	298	.230
49	.086	99	.125	149	.156	199	.183	249	.208	299	.230
50	.087	100	.126	150	.157	200	.184	250	.208	300	.231

D Option Tables

A quantity that is called the *time factor* is given in Tables D–1 to D–3. This factor when multiplied by the striking price divided by 100 gives the *time value* of puts and calls and when added to the intrinsic value, if any, gives the normal value of the option for the assumed stock price and time to expiration. Stock price P is given as a percentage of the striking price S in increments of 5% in Table D–1 and of 1% in Tables D–2 and D–3 for prices nearer the striking price. Note that the tables provide a cluster of three numbers for each entry location. The central number is the time factor for an option of average volatility and is the time value for the special case when the striking price is 100. The time value for other striking prices is $S/100$ multiplied by the time factor found from the table. Be sure you understand the distinction between time factor and time value as defined above.

The central number for an average option volatility is specifically for the volatility value $V - 0.60$. Values of V have ranged from about one-half to twice this value. We will explain later how to find the value of V for any given class of options. The values usually differ between puts and calls for any one stock. If the option volatility is higher than 0.60, the time factor must be increased, the amount for each increment of 0.10 being given by the plus number below the central value. In a similar manner, the negative value above the central number gives the amount that must be subtracted for a value of $V = 0.50$. In this manner the time value can be found for any value of V simply by adding or subtracting an amount corresponding to the number of increments of 0.10, or fraction thereof, the volatility is above or below the value 0.60. This adjustment gives correct values for one increment above or below the average in all instances, and also where the negative and positive numbers have the same absolute value, which occurs when the stock price is near the striking price.

If you want more accurate estimates for larger differences between stock price and striking price, a further adjustment can be made. As the volatility increases, the increase in time factor for each increment in V of 0.10 becomes greater, and this added amount is found by taking the difference between the absolute values (neglect algebraic signs) of the positive and negative numbers in the cluster; that is, if the cluster is

$$-1.37$$
$$5.50$$
$$+1.41$$

the time factor, for $V = 0.70$, is $5.50 + 1.41 = 6.91$ but, for $V = 0.90$, becomes $5.50 + 1.41 + (1.41 + 0.04) + (1.41 + 0.08) = 9.85$. If the value of V is less than 0.60, a similar correction can be made, but you decrease each increment following the first by twice the difference, unless marked by an *. For the number used above, and a value of $V = 0.30$, the time factor becomes $5.50 - 1.37 - (1.37 - 0.08) - (1.37 - 0.16) = 1.63$.

The time value for any option is found by multiplying the time factor, found from the table, by the striking price divided by 100. This time value is also the normal option value for out-of-the-money options, that is, for puts when the stock price is greater than the striking price and for calls when the stock price is less than the striking price. For in-the-money options, you add the intrinsic value, which is the difference between the stock price and striking price.

The discussion above assumed you knew the option volatility for the option class of interest and wanted to estimate what the normal price of a specific option would be at some future time and at some expected stock price. The tables may be used in reverse to find the option volatility from quoted option and stock prices. The most readily available prices are the daily closing prices, and you assume that the closing prices occur near the same time; but this may not be the case, and if you get a "wild" point, it is best to disregard it. For best results, use the options nearest above and below the striking price, if they are not close to expiration, and average the values. Ordinarily any recent day may be used for the near-term average; so select a date corresponding to one of the columns for time to expiration given in the table to avoid interpolation. You may assume a 90-day separation in time for the different expiration dates. The stock price will usually differ from the exact value in the table, but with increments of 1% you can choose the nearest one. If you choose to interpolate between table values, assume the variation is linear.

To find the option volatility, first subtract the intrinsic value (difference between stock price and striking price) from the quoted option price if the option is in the money—out-of-the-money options have zero intrinsic value—to find the time value. Next, divide the time value by 0.01 times the striking price. This gives the time factor, which you now compare with the cluster of numbers given in the table in the column corresponding to the time to expiration and on the line nearest the ratio of the stock price to the striking price expressed as a percentage (multiply the ratio by 100, that is, $100P/S$). The difference between the time factor in the table and the value found from the quoted data is determined, and this divided by ten times the plus or minus increment in the cluster gives the amount V should be increased or decreased from 0.60 for this option class. If the quoted value is greater than the central value of the table, use the positive increment, and if the quoted value is smaller, use the negative increment. If using options near the striking price, the second adjustment, as described in finding option values, is unnecessary, though you can use it, if you desire, following a reverse procedure to that described for finding normal option values.

You may want to determine option volatilities at points in time and form a long-term average. The values do not vary rapidly; so weekly or greater intervals may be selected. Such averages give useful information as to the trend of option premiums. Although the same tables are used for both puts and calls, remember their volatilities usually differ for any one stock and so should be determined and used separately.

Table D–1. Time factors for stock price P as a percentage of striking price S in increments of 5%. Multiply by S/100 and add intrinsic value to obtain normal value of put or call.

P/S ×100					Number of Calendar Days Until Expiration Date					
	15	30	60	90	120	150	180	210	240	270
60								*−.19	*−.25	*−.30
								.36	.50	.60
								+.27	+.34	+.40
65						*−.19	*−.25	*−.33	−.445	−.52
						.35	.50	.67	.87	1.10
						+.26	+.34	+.42	+.53	+.61
70				*−.135	*−.225	−.36	−.45	−.54	−.64	−.73
				.25	.45	.68	.93	1.20	1.50	1.75
				+.19	+.30	+.43	+.53	+.63	+.73	+.83
75			*−.13	−.28	−.40	−.52	−.64	−.76	−.87	−.98
			.23	.52	.85	1.20	1.60	1.95	2.35	2.75
			+.18	+.335	+.47	+.60	+.72	+.85	+.96	+1.07
80		*−.07	−.255	−.43	−.58	−.73	−.87	−1.00	−1.12	−1.24
		.13	.50	1.00	1.50	2.00	2.50	3.00	3.50	4.00
		+.105	+.31	+.49	+.65	+.805	+.95	+1.08	+1.20	+1.32
85	*−.05	−.185	−.42	−.62	−.80	−.97	−1.12	−1.255	−1.39	−1.52
	.08	.37	1.05	1.75	2.45	3.15	3.80	4.40	5.05	5.65
	+.07	+.22	+.47	+.68	+.86	+1.03	+1.18	+1.32	+1.45	+1.58
90	−.145	−.33	−.61	−.84	−1.035	−1.21	−1.37	−1.52	−1.66	−1.785
	.30	.87	1.95	2.95	3.85	4.70	5.50	6.25	6.95	7.65
	+.17	+.365	+.65	+.88	+1.075	+1.25	+1.405	+1.555	+1.695	+1.82
95	−.30	−.52	−.82	−1.06	−1.25	−1.425	−1.59	−1.74	−1.88	−2.015
	.95	1.90	3.45	4.70	5.78	6.75	7.70	8.55	9.35	10.10
	+.32	+.54	+.84	+1.075	+1.265	+1.44	+1.60	+1.75	+1.89	+2.03

V										
100	−.44	−.66	−.96	−1.19	−1.39	−1.57	−1.74	−1.89	−2.04	−2.17
	2.65	3.95	5.75	7.15	8.35	9.40	10.40	11.35	12.20	13.05
	+.44	+.66	+.96	+1.19	+1.39	+1.57	+1.74	+1.89	+2.04	+2.17
105	−.34	−.59	−.925	−1.18	−1.39	−1.59	−1.77	−1.93	−2.09	−2.24
	1.15	2.25	4.00	5.40	6.60	7.70	8.70	9.65	10.55	11.40
	+.36	+.61	+.94	+1.19	+1.40	+1.60	+1.78	+1.94	+2.10	+2.25
110	−.22	−.46	−.82	−1.10	−1.34	−1.545	−1.74	−1.91	−2.09	−2.25
	.53	1.35	2.85	4.15	5.32	6.40	7.40	8.35	9.25	10.12
	+.25	+.50	+.86	+1.14	+1.375	+1.58	+1.775	+1.945	+2.12	+2.28
115	−.14	−.36	−.71	−1.00	−1.25	−1.48	−1.68	−1.375	−2.05	−2.22
	.25	.87	2.13	3.30	4.40	5.40	6.40	7.35	8.25	9.10
	+.175	+.41	+.77	+1.06	−1.31	+1.54	+1.74	+1.93	+2.105	+2.275
120	*−.07	−.28	−.62	−.91	−1.16	−1.40	−1.62	−1.82	−2.01	−2.18
	.13	.57	1.60	2.70	3.70	4.65	5.60	6.55	7.40	8.25
	+.11	+.33	+.695	+.985	+1.24	+1.485	+1.70	+1.895	+2.09	+2.26
125		*−.20	−.54	−.83	−1.08	−1.33	−1.55	−1.755	−1.95	−2.14
		.40	1.25	2.20	3.15	4.07	5.00	5.85	6.75	7.60
		+.26	+.62	+.92	+1.18	−1.43	+1.65	+1.86	+2.05	+2.24
130		*−.14	−.47	−.76	−1.01	−1.26	−1.49	−1.695	−1.905	−2.10
		.27	1.00	1.85	2.70	3.60	4.45	5.30	6.15	7.00
		+.205	+.555	+.86	+1.125	+1.375	+1.61	+1.82	+2.03	+2.22
135			−.42	−.69	−.95	−1.19	−1.425	−1.64	−1.86	−2.05
			.80	1.55	2.40	3.20	4.05	4.87	5.70	6.50
			+.505	+.80	+1.07	+1.32	+1.56	+1.79	+2.00	+2.195
140			−.375	−.64	−.89	−1.14	−1.375	−1.595	−1.81	−2.02
			.65	1.35	2.10	2.90	3.70	4.50	5.30	6.10
			+.46	+.75	+1.02	+1.28	+1.52	+1.75	+1.97	+2.18

* Inaccurate for V below 0.50; use the difference between the absolute plus and minus numbers to reduce the increment to be subtracted instead of twice the difference.

163

Table D-2. Time factors for stock price P as a percentage of striking price S in increments of 1%. Multiply by S/100 to obtain value of a call; in addition, add intrinsic value for a put.

Number of Calendar Days Until Expiration Date

P/S ×100	15	30	60	90	120	150	180	210	240	270
81		* −.08	−.29	−.47	−.62	−.78	−.915	−1.05	−1.18	−1.30
		.16	.60	1.12	1.65	2.20	2.73	3.25	3.80	4.30
		+.12	+.34	+.53	+.69	+.85	+.99	+1.13	+1.255	+1.38
82		−.10	−.32	−.495	−.67	−.82	−.96	−1.10	−1.23	−1.35
		.20	.70	1.25	1.85	2.40	2.97	3.52	4.10	4.60
		+.14	+.37	+.56	+.74	+.89	+1.035	+1.175	+1.30	+1.425
83		−.14	−.35	−.535	−.71	−.87	−1.01	−1.15	−1.285	−1.41
		.25	.80	1.40	2.00	2.65	3.25	3.80	4.40	4.95
		+.17	+.405	+.60	+.78	+.935	+1.08	+1.22	+1.35	+1.48
84		−.165	−.38	−.585	−.76	−.92	−1.065	−1.205	−1.335	−1.46
		.30	.90	1.60	2.25	2.90	3.50	4.10	4.70	5.30
		+.20	+.435	+.64	+.82	+.985	+1.13	+1.27	+1.40	+1.525
85	−.05	−.185	−.42	−.62	−.80	−.97	−1.12	−1.255	−1.39	−1.52
	.08	.37	1.05	1.75	2.45	3.15	3.80	4.40	5.05	5.65
	+.07	+.22	+.47	+.68	+.86	+1.03	+1.18	+1.32	+1.45	+1.58
86	−.06	−.21	−.45	−.665	−.85	−1.01	−1.17	−1.315	−1.445	−1.575
	.12	.45	1.20	1.95	2.70	3.40	4.10	4.75	5.40	6.00
	+.085	+.245	+.50	+.72	+.91	+1.07	+1.225	+1.37	+1.50	+1.63
87	−.08	−.23	−.49	−.71	−.90	−1.06	−1.22	−1.36	−1.50	−1.63
	.15	.50	1.35	2.20	2.95	3.70	4.40	5.10	5.75	6.40
	+.105	+.27	+.54	+.76	+.96	+1.115	+1.275	+1.41	+1.55	+1.68
88	−.10	−.265	−.53	−.75	−.94	−1.11	−1.27	−1.41	−1.555	−1.68
	.18	.63	1.55	2.40	3.25	4.00	4.75	5.45	6.15	6.80
	+.125	+.30	+.575	+.80	+.99	+1.16	+1.32	+1.46	+1.60	+1.725
89	−.12	−.295	−.57	−.80	−.985	−1.16	−1.32	−1.47	−1.61	−1.73
	.23	.75	1.75	2.70	3.55	4.35	5.10	5.85	6.55	7.20
	+.145	+.33	+.615	+.84	+1.03	+1.205	+1.365	+1.51	+1.65	+1.77

90	−.145 .30 +.17	−.33 .87 +.365	−.61 1.95 +.65	−.84 2.95 +.88	−1.035 3.85 +1.075	−1.21 4.70 +1.25	−1.37 5.50 +1.405	−1.52 6.25 +1.555	−1.66 6.95 +1.695	−1.785 7.65 +1.82
91	−.17 .37 +.195	−.365 1.00 +.40	−.65 2.20 +.69	−.885 3.25 +.92	−1.08 4.20 +1.115	−1.25 5.05 −1.285	−1.42 5.90 +1.45	−1.57 6.67 +1.60	−1.71 7.40 +1.74	−1.84 8.12 +1.87
92	−.20 .48 +.225	−.40 1.20 +.43	−.70 2.50 +.73	−.93 3.60 +.96	−1.125 4.55 +1.155	−1.30 5.45 +1.33	−1.465 6.30 +1.49	−1.615 7.10 +1.64	−1.75 7.85 +1.775	−1.885 8.60 +1.91
93	−.225 .60 +.25	−.435 1.40 +.465	−.74 2.75 +.77	−.97 3.90 +1.00	−1.17 4.95 +1.195	−1.35 5.88 +1.37	−1.51 6.75 +1.53	−1.66 7.55 +1.68	−1.79 8.35 +1.81	−1.935 9.10 +1.95
94	−.26 .75 +.285	−.475 1.65 +.50	−.78 3.10 +.80	−1.02 4.30 +1.04	−1.21 5.35 +1.23	−1.39 6.30 +1.41	−1.55 7.20 +1.565	−1.70 8.05 +1.715	−1.84 8.85 +1.855	−1.975 9.60 +1.99
95	−.30 .95 +.32	−.52 1.90 +.54	−.82 3.45 +.84	−1.06 4.70 +1.075	−1.25 5.78 +1.265	−1.425 6.75 +1.44	−1.59 7.70 +1.60	−1.74 8.55 +1.75	−1.88 9.35 +1.89	−2.015 10.10 +2.03
96	−.33 1.15 +.35	−.56 2.25 +.57	−.86 3.85 +.87	−1.09 5.12 +1.10	−1.29 6.25 +1.30	−1.47 7.25 +1.48	−1.63 8.20 +1.635	−1.785 9.05 +1.79	−1.92 9.90 +1.925	−2.05 10.65 +2.06
97	−.37 1.45 +.38	−.595 2.60 +.60	−.90 4.25 +.905	−1.125 5.60 +1.13	−1.32 6.70 +1.33	−1.50 7.75 +1.505	−1.66 8.70 +1.665	−1.815 9.60 +1.82	−1.96 10.45 +1.96	−2.09 11.25 +2.09
98	−.40 1.75 +.41	−.615 3.00 +.62	−.92 4.70 +.925	−1.15 6.05 +1.155	−1.35 7.25 +1.35	−1.53 8.30 +1.53	−1.69 9.25 +1.69	−1.84 10.15 +1.84	−1.99 11.00 +1.99	−2.13 11.80 +2.13
99	−.43 2.15 +.435	−.64 3.45 +.64	−.94 5.20 +.94	−1.17 6.60 +1.17	−1.37 7.80 +1.37	−1.55 8.85 +1.55	−1.72 9.82 +1.72	−1.87 10.75 +1.87	−2.01 11.60 +2.01	−2.15 12.40 +2.15

* Inaccurate for V below 0.50; use the difference between the absolute plus and minus numbers to reduce the increment to be subtracted instead of twice the difference.

Table D–3. Time factors for stock price P as a percentage of striking price S in increments of 1%. Multiply by $S/100$ to obtain value of a put; in addition, add intrinsic value for a call.

P/S $\times 100$	Number of Calendar Days Until Expiration Date									
	15	30	60	90	120	150	180	210	240	270
101	−.435	−.66	−.97	−1.20	−1.40	−1.58	−1.75	−1.90	−2.05	−2.19
	2.20	3.50	5.30	6.75	7.95	9.00	10.00	10.95	11.85	12.70
	+.44	+.66	+.97	+1.20	+1.40	+1.585	+1.755	+1.905	+2.05	+2.19
102	−.42	−.65	−.96	−1.195	−1.405	−1.59	−1.76	−1.915	−2.07	−2.21
	1.87	3.15	4.95	6.35	7.55	8.65	9.65	10.60	11.50	12.35
	+.425	+.655	+.96	+1.20	+1.41	+1.595	+1.765	+1.92	+2.07	+2.21
103	−.40	−.63	−.95	−1.20	−1.41	−1.595	−1.765	−1.925	−2.075	−2.22
	1.58	2.80	4.60	6.00	7.20	8.30	9.30	10.25	11.15	12.00
	+.41	+.64	+.955	+1.205	+1.415	+1.60	+1.77	+1.93	+2.08	+2.225
104	−.37	−.61	−.94	−1.19	−1.40	−1.595	−1.77	−1.93	−2.08	−2.23
	1.35	2.50	4.25	5.67	6.90	8.00	9.00	9.95	10.85	11.70
	+.385	+.625	+.955	+1.20	+1.41	+1.60	+1.78	+1.935	+2.085	+2.235
105	−.34	−.59	−.925	−1.18	−1.39	−1.59	−1.77	−1.93	−2.09	−2.24
	1.15	2.25	4.00	5.40	6.60	7.70	8.70	9.65	10.55	11.40
	+.36	+.61	+.94	+1.19	+1.40	+1.60	+1.78	+1.94	+2.10	+2.25
106	−.315	−.57	−.91	−1.17	−1.39	−1.585	−1.765	−1.935	−2.095	−2.24
	.95	2.05	3.72	5.10	6.30	7.40	8.40	9.35	10.25	11.12
	+.34	+.59	+.93	+1.19	+1.405	+1.60	+1.78	+1.95	+2.11	+2.255
107	−.29	−.54	−.89	−1.15	−1.375	−1.575	−1.76	−1.94	−2.095	−2.24
	.85	1.85	3.48	4.85	6.00	7.10	8.15	9.10	10.00	10.85
	+.315	+.565	+.915	+1.17	+1.40	+1.60	+1.78	+1.955	+2.11	+2.26
108	−.26	−.51	−.86	−1.13	−1.37	−1.57	−1.76	−1.93	−2.095	−2.24
	.70	1.65	3.25	4.60	5.78	6.87	7.90	8.85	9.75	10.60
	+.29	+.545	+.89	+1.16	+1.395	+1.595	+1.78	+1.95	+2.115	+2.265
109	−.24	−.48	−.84	−1.115	−1.35	−1.56	−1.75	−1.92	−2.09	−2.24
	.60	1.50	3.05	4.35	5.55	6.63	7.65	8.60	9.50	10.35
	+.27	+.52	+.875	+1.15	+1.38	+1.59	+1.775	+1.945	+2.115	+2.265

110	−.22	−.46	−.82	−1.10	−1.34	−1.545	−1.74	−1.91	−2.09	−2.25
	.53	1.35	2.85	4.15	5.35	6.40	7.40	8.35	9.25	10.12
	+.25	+.50	+.86	+1.14	+1.375	+1.58	+1.775	+1.945	+2.12	+2.28
111	−.21	−.44	−.80	−1.08	−1.32	−1.54	−1.73	−1.91	−2.08	−2.245
	.45	1.25	2.70	3.95	5.10	6.20	7.20	8.12	9.00	9.90
	+.235	+.48	+.845	+1.125	+1.365	+1.575	+1.765	+1.95	+2.12	+2.28
112	−.19	−.42	−.78	−1.06	−1.30	−1.52	−1.72	−1.90	−2.07	−2.24
	.40	1.15	2.55	3.77	4.90	6.00	7.00	7.90	8.80	9.70
	+.22	+.46	+.825	+1.11	+1.35	+1.56	+1.76	+1.945	+2.115	+2.28
113	−.17	−.40	−.76	−1.04	−1.285	−1.50	−1.71	−1.89	−2.065	−2.23
	.35	1.05	2.40	3.60	4.70	5.80	6.80	7.70	8.60	9.50
	+.20	+.445	+.81	+1.095	+1.34	+1.55	+1.755	+1.94	+2.11	+2.27
114	−.16	−.38	−.735	−1.025	−1.27	−1.49	−1.69	−1.885	−2.06	−2.225
	.30	.95	2.25	3.45	4.55	5.60	6.60	7.50	8.40	9.30
	+.19	+.425	+.79	+1.08	+1.325	+1.545	+1.74	+1.94	+2.11	+2.27
115	−.14	−.36	−.71	−1.00	−1.25	−1.48	−1.68	−1.875	−2.05	−2.22
	.25	.87	2.13	3.30	4.40	5.40	6.40	7.35	8.25	9.10
	+.175	+.41	+.77	+1.06	+1.31	+1.54	+1.74	+1.93	+2.105	+2.275
116	*−.11	−.34	−.69	−.98	−1.235	−1.46	−1.67	−1.86	−2.04	−2.21
	.22	.80	2.00	3.15	4.25	5.25	6.20	7.15	8.05	9.90
	+.15	+.39	+.755	+1.045	+1.30	+1.525	+1.735	+1.92	+2.10	+2.27
117	*−.10	−.32	−.67	−.96	−1.22	−1.44	−1.65	−1.85	−2.03	−2.205
	.20	.73	1.90	3.00	4.10	5.10	6.05	7.00	7.87	8.75
	+.14	+.37	+.735	+1.03	+1.29	+1.51	+1.72	+1.915	+2.095	+2.27
118	*−.09	−.31	−.65	−.95	−1.20	−1.425	−1.64	−1.84	−2.02	−2.20
	.17	.67	1.80	2.90	3.95	4.95	5.90	6.85	7.70	8.57
	+.13	+.36	+.72	+1.02	+1.275	+1.50	+1.715	+1.91	+2.09	+2.255
119	*−.08	−.30	−.64	−.925	−1.18	−1.41	−1.63	−1.83	−2.015	−2.19
	.15	.62	1.70	2.80	3.80	4.80	5.75	6.70	7.55	8.40
	+.12	+.35	+.71	+1.00	+1.26	+1.49	+1.705	+1.90	+2.09	+2.25

* Inaccurate for V below 0.50; use the difference between the absolute plus and minus numbers to reduce the increment to be subtracted instead of twice the difference.

167

E References

1. Cleeton, Claud E. *The Art of Independent Investing.* Englewood Cliffs, N.J.: Prentice-Hall, 1976.
2. Hurst, J. M. *The Profit Magic of Stock Transaction Timing.* Englewood Cliffs, N.J.: Prentice-Hall, 1970.
3. The Options Clearing Corp., *Exchange Traded Put and Call Options Prospectus.* Latest edition available from any broker.
4. Crestal, Jack, and Schneider, Herman M. *Tax Planning for Investors.* Princeton, N.J.: Dow Jones & Co., Inc., 1977.

Index